United States
Department of
Agriculture

Forest Service

**Northern
Research Station**

Resource Bulletin
NRS-46

West Virginia Timber Industry: An Assessment of Timber Product Output and Use, 2007

Ronald J. Piva
Gregory W. Cook

Abstract

In 2007, there were 116 primary wood-processing mills in West Virginia, 60 fewer mills than in 2000. These mills processed 172.9 million cubic feet of industrial roundwood, of which 138.8 million cubic feet was harvested from the State. Another 50.5 million cubic feet of the industrial roundwood harvested in West Virginia was sent to primary wood-processing mills in other states and countries. Saw log harvesting accounted for 55 percent of the total harvest. The harvesting of industrial roundwood products produced 100.9 million cubic feet of logging residues. Primary wood-processing mills generated 2.1 million green tons of mill residues, with just over half of the mill residues being used by the pulpwood and particleboard industries. Only 1 percent of the mill residues generated were not being used for other products.

Cover Photo

Millyard-log deck. U.S. Forest Service.

Contents

INTRODUCTION

West Virginia's wood products manufacturing industry employs 9,400 workers with an output of more than $2.0 billion (NAICS 321—Wood product manufacturing, and NAICS 322—Paper manufacturing) (U.S. Census Bureau 2007). Given the economic importance of West Virginia's wood industry, the purpose of this bulletin is to analyze recent forest industry trends in the State and report the results of a detailed study of West Virginia's forest industry, industrial roundwood production, and associated primary mill wood and bark residue in 2007. Such detailed information is necessary for intelligent planning and decisionmaking in wood procurement, economic research, forest resources management, and forest industry development. Likewise, researchers need current forest industry and industrial roundwood information for planning projects.

In 2000, the last detailed study of all industrial roundwood output in West Virginia was conducted for the 2007 Resources Planning Act (RPA) Assessment (Smith et. al. 2009) and is used as a basis of comparison for most of this study's results. When new surveys are completed, errors and omissions from previous surveys are corrected. As a result of our ongoing efforts to improve the survey's efficiency and reliability, changes may have been made to the previous survey's data. All comparisons and analysis in this report are based on the reprocessed data from earlier surveys, which may not match earlier published data. Rows and columns of supporting tables may not sum due to rounding, but data in each table cell are accurately displayed.

Information about the forest resources of West Virginia is available at the Forest Inventory and Analysis Web site at: http://nrs.fs.fed.us/fia/data-tools/state-reports/WV

The Authors

RONALD J. PIVA, forester, received a B.S. in forest management from the University of Missouri-Columbia. He joined the Forest Service in 1987 and since then has been working with the Northern Research Station's Forest Inventory and Analysis Program.

GREGORY W. COOK, Deputy State Forester of West Virginia, received a B.S. in forestry from West Virginia University in 1980. He worked in the forest products industry for 20 years before joining the WV Division of Forestry.

STUDY METHODS

This study was a cooperative effort between the West Virginia Division of Forestry (WVDOF) and the Forest Inventory and Analysis (FIA) unit at the Northern Research Station (NRS) of the U.S. Forest Service. The FIA program is responsible for providing forest resource statistics for all ownerships across the United States, including timber product outputs.

Using questionnaires supplied by NRS and designed to determine the size and composition of the State's primary wood-using industry, its use of roundwood, and its generation and disposition of wood residues, WVDOF personnel surveyed all known primary wood-using mills. Completed questionnaires were sent to the NRS to process and analyze. As part of data processing, all industrial roundwood volumes reported on the questionnaires were converted to standard units of measure using regional conversion factors (Table 1). Timber removals by source of material and harvest residues generated during logging were estimated from standard product volumes using factors developed from logging utilization studies previously conducted by the NRS. Data on West Virginia's industrial roundwood receipts were loaded into a regional timber removals database where they were supplemented with data on out-of-State uses of West Virginia roundwood to provide a complete assessment of West Virginia's timber product output.

Certain terms used in this report -- retained, exports, imports, production, and receipts -- have specialized meanings and relationships unique to the FIA program that surveys timber product output (TPO) (Fig. 1).

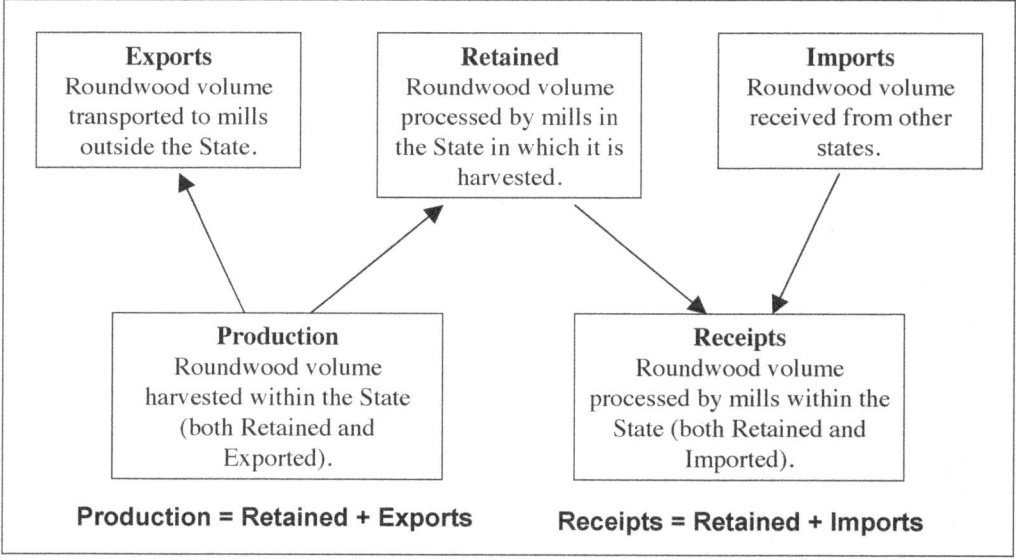

Figure 1.—Diagram of the movement of industrial roundwood.

Table 1.—Conversion factors from reported unit of measure to standard unit of measure[a]

Product and (Standard unit of measure)	Reported unit of measure					
	International 1/4-inch rule MBF	Doyle scale MBF	Green tons	Standard cords	Thousand pieces	Thousand cubic feet
Saw logs and handles (MBF International 1/4-inch rule)	1	1.38	0.2174	0.5		.158
Veneer logs and cooperage (MBF International 1/4-inch rule)	1	1.14		0.5		.158
Pulp and composite products, and industrial fuelwood (Standard cords)			0.4167	1		.085
Mine timbers (Thousand cubic feet)		0.2322		0.079	6.7	1
Poles (Pieces)	20		4.348	10	1,000	.0079
Posts (Thousand pieces)	0.2		0.04167	0.1	1	0.79
Cabin logs, excelsior/shavings, and miscellaneous products (Thousand cubic feet)	0.158	0.21804	0.0329193	0.079	7.9	1

[a] Reported volume times conversion factor = Standard volume.

PRIMARY TIMBER INDUSTRY IN WEST VIRGINIA

Industrial roundwood

- In 2007, West Virginia's primary wood-using industry included 86 sawmills, 2 veneer mills, 3 pulp and composite product mills, 10 mine timber mills, 11 post and pole mills, and 4 mills that produced other products (Table 2). There were 60 (34 percent) fewer mills in 2007 than in 2000.

- The Northeastern Forest Inventory Unit had 59 industrial roundwood processors in 2007, followed by the Southern unit with 29 industrial roundwood processors and the Northwestern unit with 28 (Fig. 2).

- In 2007, the primary wood-using mills in West Virginia processed 172.9 million cubic feet of industrial roundwood with saw logs making up nearly two-thirds of the total volume (Table 3).

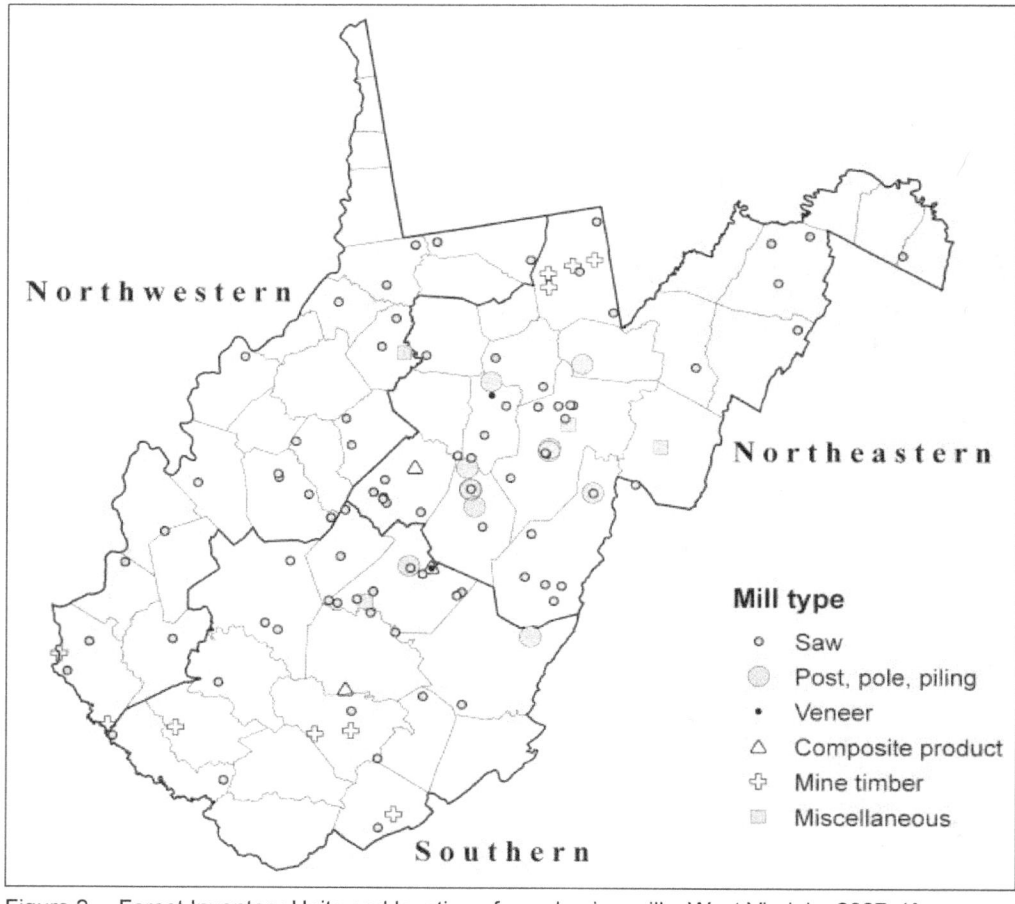

Figure 2.—Forest Inventory Units and location of wood-using mills, West Virginia, 2007. (A directory of West Virginia's forest products industry is located at: http://www.wvforestry.com/indassistance.cfm)

- Eighty percent of the industrial roundwood processed by the State's primary wood-using mills in 2007 was cut from West Virginia's forest lands. Virginia was the largest supplier of out-of-State wood for West Virginia's forest products mills, supplying 11 percent of the total industrial roundwood processed (Table 4).

- Ninety-seven percent of the industrial roundwood processed by West Virginia's primary wood-using mills were hardwood species. Yellow-poplar alone accounted for 37 percent of the total volume processed. Other important species processed were red oaks, soft maples, white oaks, hard maples, and black cherry.

- Industrial roundwood production decreased by 6 percent, from 202.0 million cubic feet in 2000 to 189.2 million cubic feet in 2007 (Table 5 and Fig. 3).

- Nearly three-quarters of the 189.2 million cubic feet of industrial roundwood harvested in West Virginia was processed by primary wood processors in the State (Table 6). Primary wood processors in Virginia received 35 percent, and Maryland received 31 percent of the industrial roundwood exported to other states. Other primary wood processors of industrial roundwood harvested in West Virginia were located in Pennsylvania, Ohio, Kentucky, Indiana, North Carolina, Wisconsin, Missouri, and other countries.

- In 2007, 42 percent (79.5 million cubic feet) of industrial roundwood was harvested from the Northeastern Forest Inventory Unit (Table 7). The Southern unit produced 39 percent (72.9 million cubic feet) and the Northwestern unit produced 19 percent (36.9 million cubic feet) of industrial roundwood harvested.

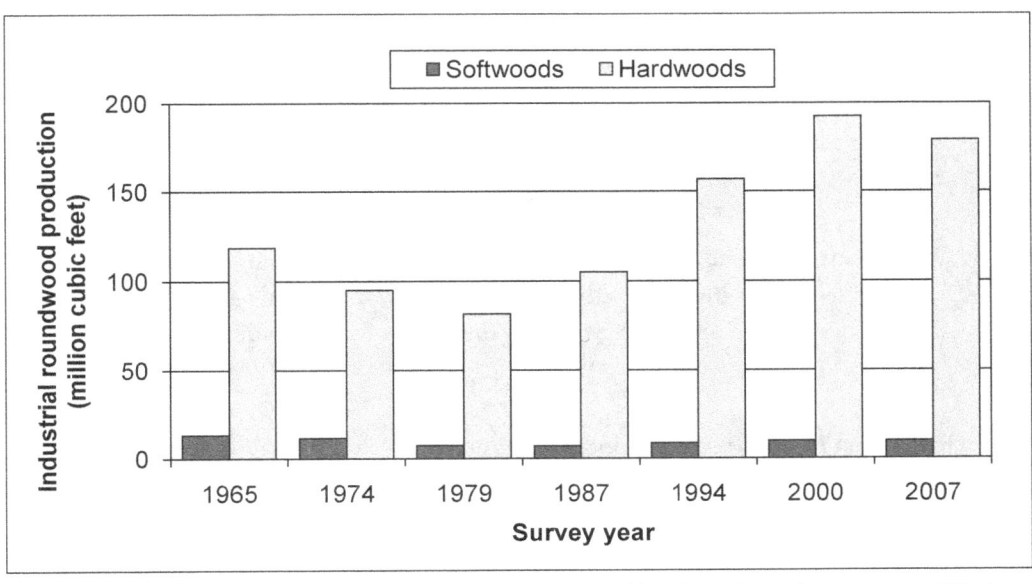

Figure 3.—Industrial roundwood production by softwoods and hardwoods, and survey year, West Virginia (Kingsley and Dickson 1968, Bones and Glover 1977, Nevel and Murriner 1979, Widmann and Murriner 1990, Widmann et al. 1998, Hansen et al. 2006).

- Yellow-poplar was the most harvested species for industrial roundwood in 2007 (Fig. 4). Other important species harvested were red oaks, white oaks, hard maples, soft maples, and black cherry.

- Harvesting for saw logs accounted for 55 percent of the total industrial roundwood produced in 2007. Pulp and composite product mills were the second largest consumers of West Virginia's industrial roundwood production, using 35 percent of the total production (Table 8 and Fig. 5).

Saw Logs

- West Virginia's sawmill receipts totaled 645.3 million board feet in 2007, a decrease of 19 percent from 2000 (Table 9). Sawmills in the Northeastern Forest Inventory Unit processed 45 percent (353.1 million board feet) of the State's total saw log receipts.

- Saw log production decreased by 22 percent between 2000 and 2007, from 803.5 million board feet in 2000 to 623.4 million board feet in 2007.

- In 2007, the red oak group accounted for almost 30 percent of the total harvest of saw logs from West Virginia's forests. Other important species groups harvested were yellow-poplar, white oaks, soft maples, hard maples, and black cherry (Fig. 6).

Other Products

- Pulpwood, at 66.7 million cubic feet, was the second most harvested product from West Virginia's forests in 2007. Pulpwood production increased by 7 percent between 2000 and 2007 (Table 5). See Piva (in prep.) for the results of a separate Northern Region pulpwood study conducted for 2007.

- Industrial roundwood harvested for veneer was the third most harvested product in West Virginia in 2007. Production of veneer logs increased from 3.7 million cubic feet in 2000 to 13.8 million cubic feet in 2007.

- Other industrial roundwood products harvested from West Virginia in 2007 were posts and fencing, mine timbers, handles, cooperage, and cabin logs. Combined, these products made up only 2 percent of the total volume of industrial roundwood produced.

- Residential fuelwood is not included in this report.

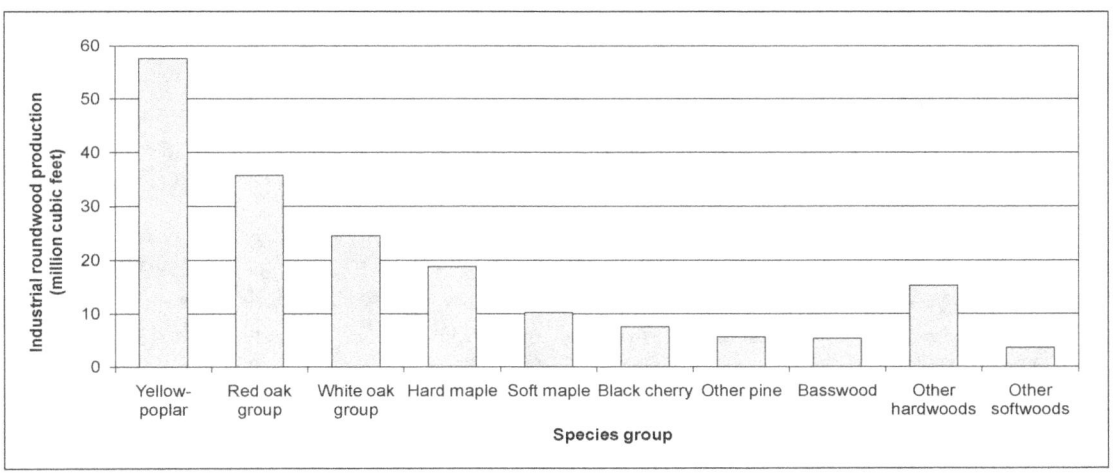

Figure 4.—Industrial roundwood production by species group, West Virginia, 2007.

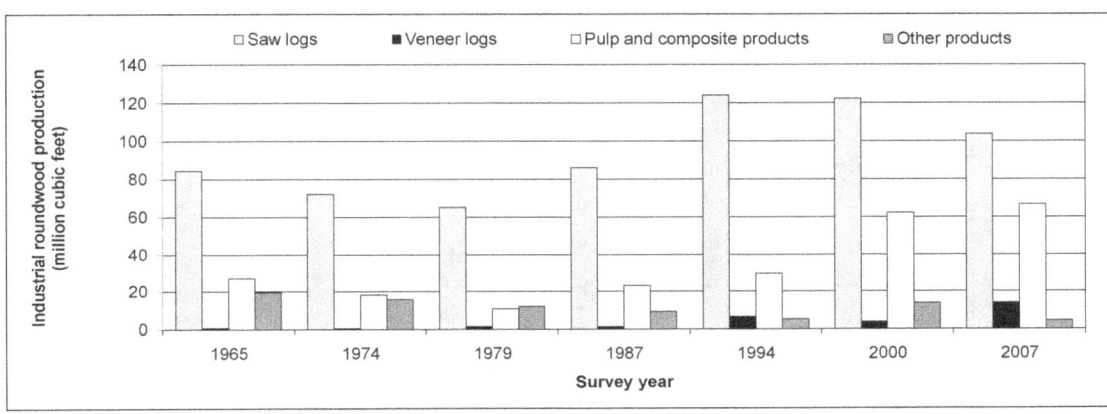

Figure 5.—Industrial roundwood production by product and survey year, West Virginia (Kingsley and Dickson 1968, Bones and Glover 1977, Nevel and Murriner 1979, Widmann and Murriner 1990, Widmann et al. 1998, Hansen et al. 2006).

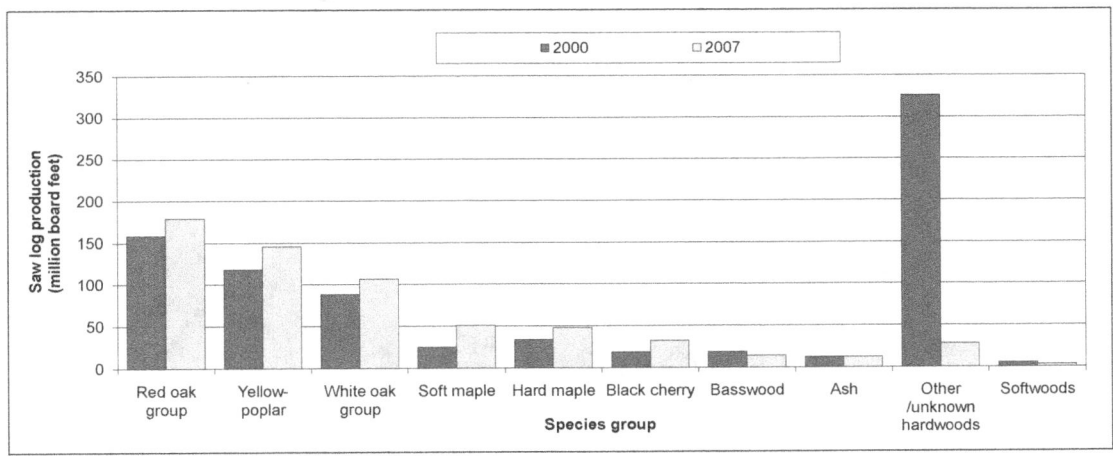

Figure 6.—Saw log production by species group, West Virginia, 2000 and 2007. (Note: Saw log production in 2000 included a large volume of unknown or mixed hardwood species that were not broken out into individual species groups. In 2007, any reported volume that was unknown or mixed hardwoods was broken out into individual species groups based on the volume of species in each county.)

Timber Removals

- During the harvest of industrial roundwood from West Virginia's forests in 2007, 189.2 million cubic feet of wood material was used for primary wood products and another 100.9 million cubic feet of wood material was left on the ground as harvest residues (Table 10 and Fig. 7).

- Growing-stock sources, at 195.5 million cubic feet, were the largest component of removals for industrial roundwood production. Eighty-three percent of the growing stock removed was used for products and 17 percent was left as harvest residue. Sawtimber-size trees accounted for 94 percent of the growing-stock volume that was used for products, and the remainder came from pole-size trees.

- In 2007, 94.7 million cubic feet of non-growing-stock wood material was removed in the production of industrial roundwood, but only 29 percent of this material was used for products, and the remainder was left on the ground as logging slash. Fifty-three percent of the non-growing-stock material used for industrial roundwood came from the limbs of growing-stock trees, and another 38 percent came from cull trees. The rest of the non-growing-stock material used for products came from dead trees, saplings, and nonforest trees.

- Forty-two percent of the total growing-stock material removed from West Virginia's timberland in 2007 came from the Northeastern Forest Inventory Unit (Table 11), followed by the Southern unit with 37 percent of the total growing-stock volume removed and the Northwestern unit with 21 percent.

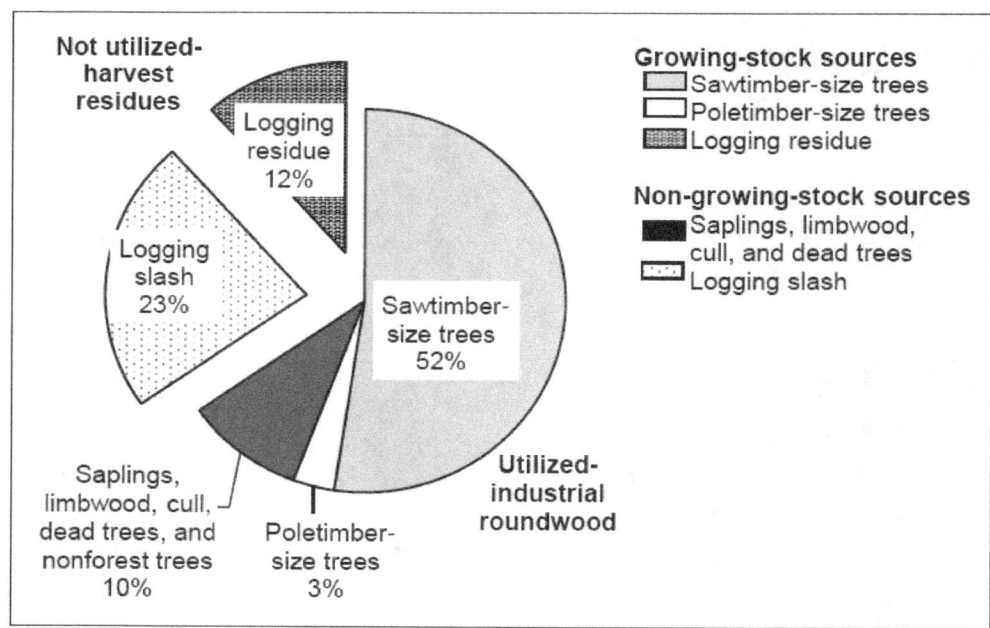

Figure 7.—Distribution of timber removals for industrial roundwood by source of material, West Virginia, 2007.

- In 2007, 957.5 million board feet was removed from West Virginia's sawtimber inventory (Table 12). Yellow-poplar, red oaks, and white oaks accounted for nearly 70 percent of the total sawtimber volume removed.

- The harvesting of industrial roundwood products from West Virginia's forests in 2007 left 100.9 million cubic feet of harvest residues on the ground (Table 13).

Harvest Intensity

- Statewide in 2007, there was an average of 52 cubic feet of average annual net growth (gross growth minus mortality) of growing stock on timberland, and an average of 25 cubic feet of harvest-related wood removals per acre of forest land. Only 13 counties had more that 30 cubic feet of total wood material removed per acre of forest land (Fig. 8). (For reference, a cord of roundwood contains about 80 cubic feet of wood.)

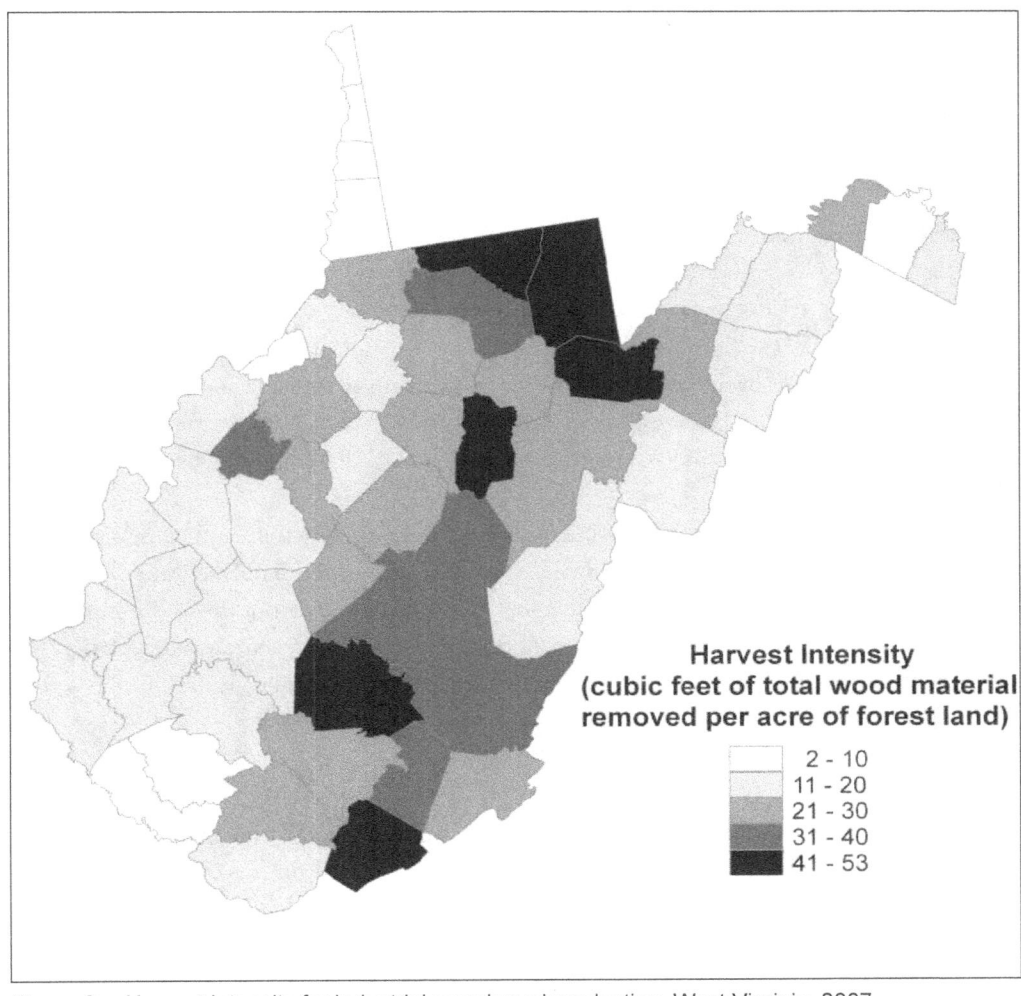

**Harvest Intensity
(cubic feet of total wood material removed per acre of forest land)**

	2 - 10
	11 - 20
	21 - 30
	31 - 40
	41 - 53

Figure 8.—Harvest intensity for industrial roundwood production, West Virginia, 2007.

- In 2007, there were 12.0 million acres of forest land in West Virginia (Widmann et al. 2010). The net volume in live trees on forest land was 26.9 billion cubic feet. The 288.9 million cubic feet of total wood material removed due to harvesting (Table 10) was 1 percent of the total live volume of trees on forest land in West Virginia.

- The Northeastern Forest Inventory Unit had the greatest harvest intensity in 2007, with an average of 27 cubic feet of total wood removals per acre of forest land. Harvesting had the greatest impact on privately owned forest land in this unit. Based on Forest Inventory and Analysis (FIA) data, private ownership accounted for 77 percent of the area of forest land but 98 percent of the average annual harvest removals (Miles 2010).

- The Southern unit had 26 cubic feet of total wood removals per acre of forest land. FIA reports that 92 percent of the forest land in this unit was privately owned, accounting for 98 percent of the average annual harvest removals.

- The Northwestern unit had 18 cubic feet of total wood removals per acre of forest land. FIA reports that 92 percent of the forest land in this unit was privately owned, accounting for 99 percent of the average annual harvest removals.

Primary Mill Residues

- In converting industrial roundwood into products, such as lumber, wood pulp, and veneer, West Virginia's primary wood-using industries generated 2.1 million green tons of wood residue (coarse and fine residues) and bark residue (Table 14).

- Fifty-two percent of the mill residues were in the form of coarse wood residue, such as slabs and edgings. Bark residue made up another 28 percent of the total mill residues produced, and fine residue accounted for the remaining 20 percent (Fig. 9).

- Fifty-two percent of the mill residues generated were used by pulp and composite product mills. Industrial fuelwood consumed 20 percent of the mill residues, mulch consumed 12 percent, and charcoal consumed 7 percent of the mill residues generated. Other minor uses for the mill residues were domestic firewood, pellets, livestock bedding, small dimension lumber, and other miscellaneous uses. Only 1 percent of the mill residues generated by the primary wood processors of West Virginia went unused (Fig. 10).

- Eighty-four percent of the coarse residue was used by pulp and composite panel mills. Industrial fuelwood consumed 37 percent of the total fine residue generated, and 43 percent of the bark residue generated was used for mulch.

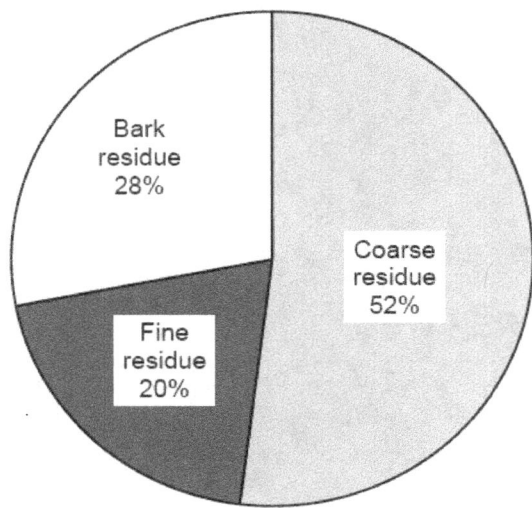

Figure 9.—Distribution of residues generated by primary wood-using mills by type of residue, West Virginia, 2007.

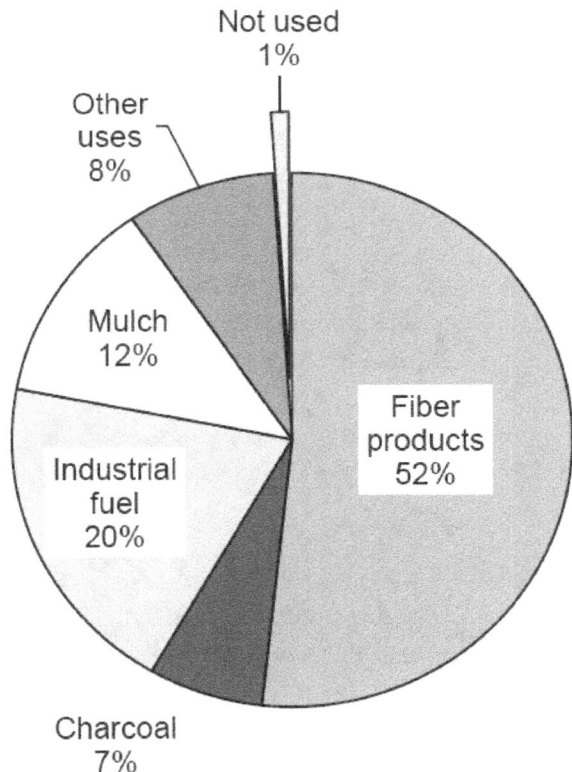

Figure 10.—Distribution of residues generated by primary wood-using mills by method of disposal, West Virginia, 2007.

ACKNOWLEDGMENTS

Special thanks are given to the primary wood-using firms for supplying information for this study and to the West Virginia Division of Forestry whose cooperation in canvassing survey respondents is greatly appreciated.

Figures 2 and 8 were created by Dale Gormanson, forester with Forest Inventory and Analysis in St. Paul, MN.

LITERATURE CITED

Bones, James T.; Glover, Ralph P., Jr. 1977. **The timber industries of West Virginia.** Resour. Bull. NE-47. Upper Darby, PA: U.S. Department of Agriculture, Forest Service, Northeastern Forest Experiment Station. 16 p.

Hansen, Bruce; Murriner, Ed; Baker, Iris; Akers, Melody. 2006. **West Virginia timber product output, 2000.** Resour. Bull. NE-165. Newtown Square, PA: U.S. Department of Agriculture, Forest Service, Northeastern Research Station 18 p.

Kingsley, Neal P.; Dickson, David R. 1968. **Timber products production in West Virginia 1965.** Resour. Bull. NE-10. Upper Darby, PA: U.S. Department of Agriculture, Forest Service, Northeastern Forest Experiment Station. 52 p.

Miles, Patrick.D. Tue Aug 24 15:50:17 CDT 2010. **Forest Inventory EVALIDator web-application version 4.01 beta.** St. Paul, MN: U.S. Department of Agriculture, Forest Service, Northern Research Station. [Available only on Internet: http://fiatools.fs.fed.us/Evalidator401/tmattribute.jsp].

Nevel, Robert L., Jr.; Murriner, Edward C. 1979. **West Virginia timber industry--periodic assessment of timber product output.** Unpublished office report. Broomall, PA: U.S. Department of Agriculture, Forest Service, Northeastern Forest Experiment Station. 70 p.

Piva, Ronald J. in prep. **Pulpwood production in the northern region, 2007.** Resour. Bull. NRS-xx. Newtown Square, PA: U.S. Department of Agriculture, Forest Service, Northern Research Station.

Smith, W. Brad; Miles, Patrick D.; Perry, Charles H.; Pugh, Scott A. 2009. **Forest resources of the United States, 2007.** Gen. Tech. Rep. WO-78. Washington, DC: U.S. Department of Agriculture, Forest Service, Washington Office. 336 p.

U. S. Census Bureau. 2007. **2007 Economic Census – Manufacturing – West Virginia.** http://factfinder.census.gov/servlet/IBQTable?_bm=y&-fds_name=EC0700A1&-geo_id=04000US54&-ds_name=EC0731A1&-_lang=en. [Accessed May 10, 2010].

Widmann, R.H.; McCaskill, G.M.; McWilliams, W.; Cook, G.W. 2010. **West Virginia's forest resources, 2007.** Res. Note NRS-60. Newtown Square, PA: U.S. Department of Agriculture, Forest Service, Northern Research Station. 5 p.

Widmann, Richard H.; Murriner, Edward C. 1990. **West Virginia timber product output-- 2004.** Resour. Bull. NRS-115. Radnor, PA: U.S. Department of Agriculture, Forest Service, Northeastern Forest Experiment Station. 20 p.

Widmann, Richard H.; Wharton, Eric H.; Murriner, Edward C. 1998. **West Virginia timber products output: 1994.** Resour. Bull. NE-143. Radnor, PA; U.S. Department of Agriculture, Forest Service, Northeastern Research Station. 15 p.

DEFINITION OF TERMS

Board foot. Unit of measure applied to roundwood. It relates to lumber that is 1 foot long, 1 foot wide, and 1 inch thick (or its equivalent).

Bolt. A short log no more than 8 feet long, to be sawn for lumber, peeled or sliced for veneer, shaved for excelsior, or converted into shingles, cooperage stock, dimension stock, blocks, blanks, or other products.

Central stem. The portion of a tree between a 1-foot stump and the minimum 4.0-inch top diameter outside bark, or point where the central stem breaks into limbs.

Coarse mill residue. Wood residue suitable for chipping such as slabs, edgings, and veneer cores.

Commercial species. Tree species presently or prospectively suitable for industrial wood products. (Note: Excludes species of typically small size, poor form, or inferior quality such as hophornbeam, Osage-orange, and redbud.)

Cull removals. Net volume of rough and rotten trees plus the net volume in sections of the central stem of growing-stock trees that do not meet regional merchantability standards but are harvested for industrial roundwood products.

Diameter at breast height (d.b.h.). The outside bark diameter at 4.5 feet above the forest floor on the uphill side of the tree. For determining breast height, the forest floor includes the duff layer that may be present, but does not include unincorporated woody debris that may rise above the ground line.

Doyle rule. A simple log rule or formula for estimating the board-foot volume of logs based on a 4-inch slabbing allowance to square the log. This rule is used in the Eastern and Southern United States.

Exports. The volume of roundwood utilized by mills outside the state where the timber was harvested.

Fine mill residue. Wood residue not suitable for chipping, such as sawdust and veneer clippings.

Forest land. Land at least 10-percent stocked with trees of any size, or formerly having had such tree cover, and not currently developed for nonforest use. (Note: Stocking is measured by comparing specified standards with basal area and/or number of trees, age or size, and spacing.) The minimum area for classification of forest land is 1 acre. Roadside, streamside, and shelterbelt strips of timber must have a crown width of at least 120 feet to qualify as forest land. Unimproved roads and trails, streams or other bodies of water, or clearings in forest areas shall be classified as forest if less than 120 feet wide.

Growing-stock removals. The growing-stock volume removed from timberland by harvesting industrial roundwood products. (Note: Includes sawtimber removals, poletimber removals, and logging residues.)

Growing-stock tree. A live timberland tree of commercial species that meets specified standards of size, quality, and merchantability. (Note: Excludes rough, rotten, and dead trees.)

Growing-stock volume. Net volume of growing-stock trees 5.0 inches d.b.h. and larger, from 1 foot above the ground to a minimum 4.0-inch top diameter outside bark of the central stem or to the point where the central stem breaks into limbs.

Hardwoods. Dicotyledonous trees, usually broad-leaved and deciduous.

Harvest residues. The total net volume of unused portions of trees cut or killed by logging. (Note: Includes both logging residues and logging slash.)

Industrial fuelwood. A roundwood product, with or without bark, used to generate energy at manufacturing facilities and schools, correctional institutions, or electric generating plants.

Imports. The volume of roundwood delivered to a mill or group of mills in a specific state but harvested outside that state.

Industrial roundwood exports. The quantity of industrial roundwood harvested in a geographical area and transported to other geographical areas.

Industrial roundwood imports. The quantity of industrial roundwood received from other geographical areas.

Industrial roundwood products. Saw logs, pulpwood, veneer logs, poles, commercial posts, pilings, cooperage logs, particleboard bolts, shaving bolts, lath bolts, charcoal bolts, and chips from roundwood used for pulp or board products.

Industrial roundwood production. The quantity of industrial roundwood harvested in a geographic area plus all industrial roundwood exported to other geographical areas.

Industrial roundwood receipts. The quantity of industrial roundwood received by commercial mills in a geographic area plus all industrial roundwood imported from other geographical areas.

Industrial roundwood retained. The quantity of industrial roundwood harvested from and processed by commercial mills within the same geographical area.

International 1/4-inch rule. A log rule or formula for estimating the board-foot volume of logs, allowing ½ inch of taper for each 4-foot length and assuming ¼ inch of kerf. This rule is used as the U.S. Forest Service standard log rule in the Eastern United States.

Limbwood removals. Net volume of all portions of a tree other than the central stem (including forks, large limbs, tops, and stumps) harvested for industrial roundwood products.

Logging residue. The net volume of unused portions of the merchantable central stem of growing-stock trees cut or killed by logging.

Logging slash. The net volume of unused portions of the unmerchantable (non-growing stock) sections of trees cut or killed by logging.

Merchantable sections. Refers to sections of the central stem of growing-stock trees that meet either pulpwood or saw log specifications.

Net volume. Gross volume less deductions for rot, sweep, or other defects affecting use for roundwood products.

Noncommercial species. Trees species of typically small size, poor form, or inferior quality that normally do not develop into trees suitable for industrial roundwood products. Noncommercial species are listed in the volume tables as rough trees.

Nonforest land. Land that has never supported forests, and land formerly forested where use for timber management is precluded by development for other uses. (Note: Includes areas used for crops, active Christmas tree plantations, orchards, nurseries, improved pasture, residential areas, city parks, improved roads of any width and adjoining clearings, powerline clearings of any width, and 1- to 39.9-acre areas of water classified by the Bureau of the Census as land.) If intermingled in forest areas, unimproved roads and nonforest strips must be more than 120 feet wide and more than 1 acre to qualify as nonforest land.

Nonforest land removals. Net volume of trees on nonforest lands harvested for industrial roundwood products.

Poletimber. A growing-stock tree at least 5.0 inches d.b.h. but smaller than sawtimber size (9.0 inches d.b.h. for softwoods, 11.0 inches d.b.h. for hardwoods).

Poletimber removals. Net volume in the merchantable central stem of poletimber trees harvested for industrial roundwood products.

Primary wood-using mills. Mills receiving roundwood or chips from roundwood for processing into products such as lumber, veneer, and pulp.

Primary wood-using mill residue. Wood materials (coarse and fine) and bark generated at manufacturing plants that process industrial roundwood into principal products. These residues include wood products obtained incidental to production of principal products and wood materials not utilized for some product.

Production. The quantity of roundwood material harvested in a geographic area plus all roundwood material exported to other geographical areas.

Receipts. The quantity of roundwood material received by commercial mills in a geographic area plus all roundwood material imported from other geographical areas.

Retained. Roundwood volume harvested from and processed by mills within the same state.

Rotten tree. A tree that does not meet regional merchantability standards because of excessive unsound cull.

Rough tree. A tree that does not meet regional merchantability standards because of excessive sound cull (includes forks, sweep and crook, and large branches or knots), including noncommercial tree species.

Roundwood. Logs, bolts, or other round sections cut from trees (including chips from roundwood).

Sapling. A live tree between 1.0 and 5.0 inches d.b.h.

Saw log portion. That portion of the central stem of sawtimber trees between the stump and the saw log top.

Saw log top. The point on the central stem of sawtimber trees above which a saw log cannot be produced. The minimum saw log top is 7.0 inches diameter outside bark for softwoods and 9.0 inches diameter outside bark for hardwoods.

Sawtimber removals. As used in Table 10, sawtimber removals refers to the net volume in the merchantable central stem of sawtimber-size trees harvested for industrial roundwood products. (Note: includes the saw log and upper stem portions of sawtimber-size trees.) When referring to the sawtimber volume removed from timberland as in Table 12, sawtimber removals refers to the net volume in the saw log portion of sawtimber-size trees harvested for roundwood products or left on the ground as harvest residue, and is usually expressed in thousands of board feet (International 1/4-inch rule).

Sawtimber tree. A growing-stock tree containing at least a 12-foot saw log or two noncontiguous saw logs 8 feet or longer, and meeting regional specifications for freedom from defect. Softwoods must be at least 9.0 inches d.b.h. and hardwoods must be at least 11.0 inches d.b.h.

Sawtimber volume. Net volume in the saw log portion of sawtimber trees.

Softwoods. Coniferous trees, usually evergreen, having needles or scale-like leaves.

Timber product output. The volume of roundwood products produced from an area's forests.

Timberland. Forest land that is producing, or is capable of producing, in excess of 20 cubic feet per acre per year of industrial roundwood products under natural conditions, is not withdrawn from timber utilization by statute or administrative regulation, and is not associated with urban or rural development.

Tree. A woody perennial plant, typically large, with a single well-defined stem carrying a more or less definite crown; sometimes defined as attaining a minimum diameter of 3 in. (7.6 cm) and a minimum height of 15 ft (4.6 m) at maturity. For FIA, any plant on the tree list in the current field manual is measured as a tree.

Upper stem portion. That portion of the central stem of sawtimber trees between the saw log top and the minimum top diameter of 4.0 inches outside bark, or to the point where the central stem breaks into limbs.

COMMON AND SCIENTIFIC NAMES OF TREE SPECIES BY SPECIES GROUP

Softwoods

Cedars
    Atlantic white-cedar   *Chamaecyparis thyoides*
    Eastern redcedar   *Juniperus virginiana*
Balsam fir   *Abies balsamea*
Eastern hemlock   *Tsuga canadensis*
Shortleaf pine   *Pinus echinata*
Loblolly pine   *Pinus taeda*
Red pine   *Pinus resinosa*
White pine   *Pinus strobus*
Other pines
    Table Mountain pine   *Pinus pungens*
    Pitch pine   *Pinus rigida*
    Scotch pine   *Pinus sylvestris*
    Virginia pine   *Pinus virginiana*
Spruce
    Norway spruce   *Picea abies*
    White spruce   *Picea glauca*
    Red spruce   *Picea rubens*

Hardwoods

Ash
    White ash   *Fraxinus americana*
    Black ash   *Fraxinus nigra*
    Green ash   *Fraxinus pennsylvanica*
Aspen/balsam poplar
    Bigtooth aspen   *Populus grandidentata*
    Quaking aspen   *Populus tremuloides*
Basswood
    American basswood   *Tilia americana*
    White basswood   *Tilia heterophylla*
American beech   *Fagus grandifolia*
Yellow birch   *Betula alleghaniensis*
Other birches
    Sweet birch   *Betula lenta*
    River birch   *Betula nigra*
Black cherry   *Prunus serotina*
Black walnut   *Juglans nigra*
Elm
    Winged elm   *Ulmus alata*
    American elm   *Ulmus americana*
    Slippery elm   *Ulmus rubra*

Hickory
    Mockernut hickory   *Carya alba*
    Bitternut hickory   *Carya cordiformis*
    Pignut hickory   *Carya glabra*
    Shellbark hickory   *Carya laciniosa*
    Shagbark hickory   *Carya ovata*
Hard maples
    Black maple   *Acer nigrum*
    Sugar maple   *Acer saccharum*
Soft maples
    Boxelder   *Acer negundo*
    Striped maple   *Acer pensylvanicum*
    Red maple   *Acer rubrum*
    Silver maple   *Acer saccharinum*
    Mountain maple   *Acer spicatum*
Red oak group
    Scarlet oak   *Quercus coccinea*
    Southern red oak   *Quercus falcata*
    Shingle oak   *Quercus imbricaria*
    Pin oak   *Quercus palustris*
    Northern red oak   *Quercus rubra*
    Black oak   *Quercus velutina*
White oak group
    White oak   *Quercus alba*
    Swamp white oak   *Quercus bicolor*
    Swamp chestnut oak   *Quercus michauxii*
    Chinkapin oak   *Quercus muehlenbergii*
    Chestnut oak   *Quercus prinus*
    Post oak   *Quercus stellata*
Sweetgum   *Liquidambar styraciflua*
American sycamore   *Platanus occidentalis*
Yellow-poplar   *Liriodendron tulipifera*
Other hardwoods
    Ohio buckeye   *Aesculus glabra*
    Yellow buckeye   *Aeseulus octandra*
    Common serviceberry   *Amelanchier arborea*
    American hornbeam   *Carpinus caroliniana*
    American chestnut   *Castanea dentata*
    Northern catalpa   *Catalpa speciosa*
    Hackberry   *Celtis occidentalis*
    Eastern redbud   *Cercis canadensis*
    Flowering dogwood   *Cornus florida*
    Hawthorn spp.   *Crataegus spp.*
    Common persimmon   *Diospyros virginiana*
    Honeylocust   *Gleditsia triacanthos*
    Butternut   *Juglans cinerea*

Cucumbertree	*Magnolia acuminata*
Mountain or Fraser magnolia	*Magnolia fraseri*
Umbrella magnolia	*Magnolia tripetala*
Apple spp.	*Malus spp.*
Blackgum	*Nyssa sylvatica*
Eastern hophornbeam	*Ostrya virginiana*
Sourwood	*Oxydendrum arboreum*
Paulownia, empress-tree	*Paulownia tomentosa*
Pin cherry	*Prunus pensylvanica*
Chokecherry	*Prunus virginiana*
Black locust	*Robinia pseudoacacia*
Black willow	*Salix nigra*
Sassafras	*Sassafras albidum*
American mountain-ash	*Sorbus americana*

TABLES

Table 1.—Conversion factors from reported unit of measure to standard unit of measure (This table is in the Study Methods section.)

Table 2.—Number of active primary wood-using mills by mill type and survey year, West Virginia

Table 3.—Industrial roundwood receipts in thousand cubic feet, by mill type, hardwoods and softwoods, and survey year, West Virginia

Table 4.—Industrial roundwood receipts in thousand cubic feet, by Forest Inventory Unit, species group, and State of origin, West Virginia, 2007

Table 5.—Industrial roundwood production in thousand cubic feet, by product, hardwoods and softwoods, and survey year, West Virginia

Table 6.—Industrial roundwood production in thousand cubic feet, by Forest Inventory Unit, species group, and State of destination, West Virginia, 2007

Table 7.—Industrial roundwood production in thousand cubic feet, by Forest Inventory Unit, county, and species group, West Virginia, 2007

Table 8.—Industrial roundwood production by Forest Inventory Unit, species group, and product, West Virginia, 2007

Table 9.—Saw log receipts and production in thousand board feet, International 1/4-inch rule, by Forest Inventory Unit and species group, West Virginia, 2000 and 2007

Table 10.—Wood material harvested for industrial roundwood in thousand cubic feet, by Forest Inventory Unit, source of material, and species group, West Virginia, 2007

Table 11.—Growing-stock removals from timberland for industrial roundwood in thousand cubic feet, by Forest Inventory Unit, county, and species group, West Virginia, 2007

Table 12.—Sawtimber removals from timberland for industrial roundwood in thousand board feet, International 1/4-inch rule, by Forest Inventory Unit, county, and species group, West Virginia, 2007

Table 13.—Harvest residue generated by industrial roundwood harvesting in thousand cubic feet, by Forest Inventory Unit, county, and species group, West Virginia, 2007

Table 14.—Disposition of residues produced at primary wood-using mills in thousand tons, green weight, by Forest Inventory Unit, disposition, residue type, and softwoods and hardwoods, West Virginia, 2007

Table 2. -- Number of active primary wood-using mills by mill type and survey year, West Virginia[a]

Kind of mill and mill size		Survey Year						
		1965	1974[b]	1979[b]	1987	1994	2000[b]	2007
Sawmills	Large[c]	16	--	--	30	51	--	38
	Medium[d]	117	90	77	81	62	90	16
	Small[e]	372	137	124	53	64	82	32
	Total	505[g]	365	201	164	177	172	86
Veneer mills		NA	4	NA	1	2	2	2
Pulp and composite product mills		0	0	0	0	0	2	3
Mine timbers		NA	NA	NA	NA	NA	NA	10
Post and pole mills		NA	NA	NA	NA	NA	NA	11
Other products[f]		NA	NA	NA	NA	NA	NA	4
All mills		505	269	201	165	179	176	116

[a] Mills that produce more than one product are only counted for the product they process the most of.
[b] Large saw mills are included in medium sawmills.
[c] Annual lumber production in excess of 5 million board feet.
[d] Annual lumber production from 1 million to 5 million board feet.
[e] Annual lumber production less than 1 million board feet.
[f] Includes plants producing mulch, mine timbers, excelsior, shavings, etc.
[g] Approximate.
NA Not available.

Table 3.--Industrial roundwood receipts in thousand cubic feet, by mill type, hardwoods and softwoods, and survey year, West Virginia

Kind of mill	Survey Year						
	1965	1974	1987	1994	2000	2007
ALL SPECIES						
Saw logs	71,606	65,986	78,909	107,059	116,849	107,207
Pulpwood and composite	NA	NA	NA	NA	NA	44,320
Mine timbers	NA	NA	NA	NA	NA	1,664
Posts/fencing	NA	NA	NA	NA	NA	2,917
Other products[a]	NA	NA	NA	NA	NA	16,765
Total						172,872
SOFTWOODS						
Saw logs	3,168	2,506	725	1,241	546	345
Pulpwood and composite	NA	NA	NA	NA	NA	2,996
Mine timbers	NA	NA	NA	NA	NA	574
Posts/fencing	NA	NA	NA	NA	NA	1,398
Other products[a]	NA	NA	NA	NA	NA	49
Total						5,363
HARDWOODS						
Saw logs	68,621	63,621	78,207	105,865	116,303	106,861
Pulpwood and composite	NA	NA	NA	NA	NA	41,323
Mine timbers	NA	NA	NA	NA	NA	1,090
Posts/fencing	NA	NA	NA	NA	NA	1,518
Other products[a]	NA	NA	NA	NA	NA	16,716
Total						167,509

[a] Includes plants producing veneer, cooperage, handles, cabin logs, etc.
All table cells without observations are indicated by -- . Table value of 0 indicates the volume rounds to less than 1 thousand cubic feet. Columns and rows may not add to their totals due to rounding.

Table 4. -- Industrial roundwood receipts in thousand cubic feet, by Forest Inventory Unit, species group, and State of origin, West Virginia, 2007

ALL UNITS

Species group	Total	Kentucky	Maryland	North Carolina	Ohio	Pennsylvania	South Carolina	Tennessee	Virginia	West Virginia
Softwoods										
Eastern redcedar	0	--	--	--	--	--	--	--	0	0
Hemlock	445	--	--	--	--	--	--	--	5	440
Loblolly/shortleaf pine	280	2	--	94	8	--	7	--	77	91
Red pine	123	12	16	0	54	16	--	--	25	--
White pine	3,288	72	2	0	277	87	--	2	1,179	1,669
Other pine	1,031	72	2	0	246	44	--	--	204	463
Spruce	196	--	--	--	--	--	--	--	32	164
Softwood total	5,363	157	20	95	585	148	7	2	1,522	2,827
Hardwoods										
Ash	2,324	19	--	1	68	--	0	0	339	1,896
Aspen/balsam poplar	629	37	2	--	163	123	--	--	45	259
Basswood	4,880	143	141	5	108	55	1	1	407	4,019
Beech	1,922	20	1	24	4	--	--	6	277	1,589
Yellow birch	400	9	--	0	1	2	0	0	71	315
Other birch	1,492	36	36	2	6	28	0	0	113	1,270
Black cherry	5,979	21	39	--	33	37	--	2	930	4,916
Black walnut	392	19	--	--	9	--	--	1	60	303
Cottonwood	70	4	--	--	60	1	--	--	5	--
Elm	781	35	39	0	146	71	--	0	52	437
Hickory	2,361	32	1	5	12	--	1	1	299	2,011
Hard maple	8,640	50	34	3	100	41	0	1	1,110	7,300
Soft maple	18,819	368	531	74	610	881	--	19	1,948	14,388
Red oak group	31,599	364	119	11	473	145	1	2	3,260	27,224
White oak group	18,391	151	59	12	335	77	2	2	2,026	15,726
Sweetgum	7	1	--	--	3	--	--	--	1	3
Sycamore	751	27	27	0	94	12	0	0	50	541
Tupelo/gum	443	16	22	1	37	20	0	0	38	309
Yellow-poplar	64,482	1,979	390	313	2,086	897	--	80	7,666	51,071
Other hardwoods	3,151	101	120	4	198	145	1	1	212	2,370
Hardwood total	167,509	3,433	1,561	457	4,546	2,535	6	117	18,909	135,946
State total	172,872	3,590	1,581	552	5,131	2,682	13	120	20,431	138,773

NORTHEASTERN

					State of origin					
Species group	Total	Kentucky	Maryland	North Carolina	Ohio	Pennsyl-vania	South Carolina	Tennessee	Virginia	West Virginia
Softwoods										
Eastern redcedar	0	--	--	--	--	--	--	--	0	0
Hemlock	205	--	--	--	--	--	--	--	5	200
Loblolly/shortleaf pine	53	2	--	--	8	--	--	--	15	28
Red pine	123	12	16	0	54	16	--	--	25	--
White pine	1,233	65	2	0	277	87	--	--	252	550
Other pine	957	72	2	0	246	44	--	--	204	388
Spruce	136	--	--	--	--	--	--	--	32	104
Softwood total	2,707	151	20	1	585	148	--	--	533	1,271
Hardwoods										
Ash	1,151	--	--	--	--	--	--	--	208	944
Aspen/balsam poplar	589	34	2	--	162	123	--	--	45	223
Basswood	3,019	64	141	--	88	52	--	--	217	2,456
Beech	492	--	1	--	--	--	--	--	91	400
Yellow birch	218	--	--	--	--	--	--	--	65	153
Other birch	1,290	35	36	--	5	28	--	--	94	1,091
Black cherry	3,643	--	39	--	--	37	--	--	701	2,867
Black walnut	100	--	--	--	--	--	--	--	19	81
Cottonwood	70	4	--	--	60	1	--	--	5	--
Elm	749	35	39	--	146	71	--	--	51	407
Hickory	1,233	--	1	--	--	--	--	--	222	1,010
Hard maple	4,728	--	34	--	--	37	--	--	873	3,784
Soft maple	11,632	266	531	--	535	878	--	--	1,152	8,271
Red oak group	13,746	--	119	--	--	107	--	--	2,091	11,429
White oak group	7,904	--	59	--	--	62	--	--	1,320	6,463
Sweetgum	7	1	--	--	3	--	--	--	1	3
Sycamore	652	27	27	--	93	12	--	--	48	445
Tupelo/gum	385	16	22	--	36	20	--	--	33	257
Yellow-poplar	27,946	468	390	--	1,598	701	--	--	3,501	21,287
Other hardwoods	2,686	98	120	--	197	145	--	--	179	1,949
Hardwood total	82,237	1,048	1,561	--	2,923	2,273	--	--	10,914	63,519
Unit total	84,945	1,198	1,581	1	3,508	2,421	--	--	11,446	64,789

(Table 4 continued on next page)

25

(Table 4 continued)

26

SOUTHERN

Species group	Total		State of origin							
		Kentucky	Maryland	North Carolina	Ohio	Pennsylvania	South Carolina	Tennessee	Virginia	West Virginia
Softwoods										
Hemlock	240	--	--	--	--	--	--	--	--	240
Loblolly/shortleaf pine	227	--	--	94	--	--	--	7	62	63
White pine	2,033	7	--	--	--	--	--	2	927	1,097
Other pine	54	--	--	--	--	--	--	--	--	54
Spruce	59	--	--	--	--	--	--	--	--	59
Softwood total	2,613	7	--	94	--	--	--	7	989	1,513
Hardwoods										
Ash	770	19	--	1	6	--	0	0	131	611
Aspen/balsam poplar	39	3	--	--	0	1	--	--	--	35
Basswood	1,741	79	--	5	1	3	1	1	190	1,462
Beech	1,329	20	--	24	4	--	--	6	185	1,088
Yellow birch	182	9	--	0	1	--	0	0	7	162
Other birch	196	1	--	2	--	2	--	--	18	174
Black cherry	1,883	21	--	--	4	--	--	2	230	1,626
Black walnut	258	19	--	--	6	--	--	1	41	191
Elm	23	0	--	0	0	--	--	0	1	21
Hickory	914	32	--	5	6	--	1	1	78	792
Hard maple	3,156	50	--	3	11	--	0	1	238	2,854
Soft maple	6,432	102	--	74	17	--	--	19	796	5,423
Red oak group	13,678	364	--	11	58	--	1	2	1,169	12,072
White oak group	7,477	151	--	12	22	--	2	2	707	6,580
Sycamore	48	0	--	0	0	--	0	0	2	46
Tupelo/gum	56	0	--	1	0	--	--	0	5	50
Yellow-poplar	33,508	1,511	--	313	200	159	--	80	4,165	27,080
Other hardwoods	455	3	--	4	0	--	1	1	33	412
Hardwood total	72,144	2,385	--	457	339	165	6	117	7,995	60,680
Unit total	74,757	2,392	--	551	339	165	13	120	8,984	62,193

NORTHWESTERN

		State of origin								
Species group	Total	Kentucky	Maryland	North Carolina	Ohio	Pennsylvania	South Carolina	Tennessee	Virginia	West Virginia
Softwoods										
White pine	22	--	--	--	--	--	--	--	--	22
Other pine	21	--	--	--	--	--	--	--	--	21
Softwood total	43	--	--	--	--	--	--	--	--	43
Hardwoods										
Ash	403	--	--	--	61	--	--	--	--	341
Aspen/balsam poplar	1	--	--	--	--	--	--	--	--	1
Basswood	121	--	--	--	19	--	--	--	--	102
Beech	101	--	--	--	0	--	--	--	--	101
Other birch	6	--	--	--	1	--	--	--	--	5
Black cherry	452	--	--	--	29	--	--	--	--	423
Black walnut	33	--	--	--	3	--	--	--	--	30
Elm	10	--	--	--	0	--	--	--	--	10
Hickory	215	--	--	--	6	--	--	--	--	209
Hard maple	756	--	--	--	90	4	--	--	--	663
Soft maple	755	--	--	--	59	4	--	--	--	693
Red oak group	4,175	--	--	--	415	38	--	--	--	3,723
White oak group	3,010	--	--	--	313	15	--	--	--	2,683
Sycamore	51	--	--	--	0	--	--	--	--	51
Tupelo/gum	2	--	--	--	0	--	--	--	--	2
Yellow-poplar	3,027	--	--	--	287	36	--	--	--	2,704
Other hardwoods	10	--	--	--	1	--	--	--	--	9
Hardwood total	13,128	--	--	--	1,284	96	--	--	--	11,748
Unit total	13,171	--	--	--	1,284	96	--	--	--	11,791

All table cells without observations are indicated by --. Table value of 0 indicates the volume rounds to less than 1 thousand cubic feet. Columns and rows may not add to their totals due to rounding.

27

Table 5.--Industrial roundwood production in thousand cubic feet, by product, hardwoods and softwoods, and survey year, West Virginia

Product	Survey Year							
	1965	1974	1979	1987[a]	1994	2000	2007
ALL SPECIES							
Saw logs	84,455	72,242	65,100	86,100	124,149	122,329	104,422
Veneer logs	791	491	1,300	1,200	6,538	3,735	13,760
Pulpwood	27,141	18,156	10,700	23,120	29,605	62,229	66,657
Cooperage	761	492	--	--	--	--	80
Mine timbers	11,012	6,742	--	--	--	--	1,361
Post, poles, and pilings	2,681	--	--	--	--	--	2,681
Other products[b]	5,145	8,488	12,100	9,149	5,080	13,686	288
Total	131,986	106,611	89,200	119,569	165,372	201,979	189,249
SOFTWOODS							
Saw logs	3,584	2,887	3,000	1,000	2,633	767	520
Veneer logs	--	--	--	--	--	--	0
Pulpwood	8,696	4,318	2,500	5,899	5,559	7,776	7,472
Cooperage	--	--	--	--	--	--	--
Mine timbers	898	550	--	--	--	--	345
Post, poles, and pilings	40	--	--	--	--	--	1,239
Other products[b]	--	3,884	1,900	5	234	1,072	38
Total	13,218	11,639	7,400	6,904	8,426	9,615	9,614
HARDWOODS							
Saw logs	80,871	69,355	62,100	85,100	121,516	121,562	103,902
Veneer logs	791	491	1,300	1,200	6,538	3,735	13,760
Pulpwood	18,445	13,838	8,200	17,221	24,046	54,453	59,186
Cooperage	761	492	--	--	--	--	80
Mine timbers	10,114	6,192	--	--	--	--	1,016
Post, poles, and pilings	2,641	--	--	--	--	--	1,442
Other products[b]	5,145	4,604	10,200	1,483	1,372	12,614	249
Total	118,768	94,972	81,800	105,004	156,946	192,364	179,635

[a] 1987 saw log and veneer totals were recalculated using the same board foot to cubic foot conversion as all other years.
[b] Includes plants producing handles, excelsior, shavings, cabin logs, etc. For 1979, 1987, 1994, and 2000, includes cooperage. mine timber. and post. poles. and pilings.
All table cells without observations are indicated by -- . Table value of 0 indicates the volume rounds to less than 1 thousand cubic feet. Columns and rows may not add to their totals due to rounding.

28

Table 6. -- Industrial roundwood production in thousand cubic feet, by Forest Inventory Unit, species group, and State of destination, West Virginia, 2007

ALL UNITS

Species group	Total	Indiana	Kentucky	Maryland	Missouri	North Carolina	Ohio	Pennsylvania	Virginia	West Virginia	Wisconsin	Other countries
Softwoods												
Eastern redcedar	0	--	--	--	--	0	--	--	--	0	--	--
Hemlock	703	--	--	136	--	--	1	9	117	440	--	--
Loblolly/shortleaf pine	209	--	--	36	--	--	75	1	5	91	--	--
Red pine	8	--	--	2	--	--	--	--	6	--	--	--
White pine	2,887	--	--	373	--	--	743	10	92	1,669	--	--
Other pine	5,594	--	--	1,300	--	--	3,605	4	222	463	--	--
Spruce	213	--	--	8	--	--	--	--	41	164	--	--
Softwood total	9,614	--	--	1,856	--	0	4,424	25	482	2,827	--	--
Hardwoods												
Ash	2,926	2	1	361	--	6	72	147	390	1,896	--	52
Aspen/balsam poplar	331	--	--	64	--	--	8	0	--	259	--	--
Basswood	5,334	--	--	517	--	--	57	178	563	4,019	--	--
Beech	2,778	--	0	427	--	--	55	64	643	1,589	0	--
Yellow birch	812	0	--	253	--	--	2	16	225	315	--	--
Other birch	2,010	--	--	289	--	--	3	23	425	1,270	--	--
Black cherry	7,672	79	--	1,067	--	67	84	387	914	4,916	1	157
Black walnut	560	29	191	--	--	16	6	15	0	303	0	0
Elm	624	--	--	106	--	--	40	6	34	437	--	--
Hickory	3,877	10	0	671	--	1	136	147	890	2,011	10	184
Soft maple	10,290	24	--	1,072	--	13	154	601	930	7,300	14	--
Hard maple	18,934	9	0	1,718	--	--	169	635	1,757	14,388	--	259
Red oak group	35,851	33	247	2,070	--	16	500	2,212	3,184	27,224	43	321
White oak group	24,591	13	683	2,704	43	23	493	1,260	3,301	15,726	--	346
Sweetgum	3	--	--	--	--	--	--	--	--	3	--	--
Sycamore	735	--	--	126	--	--	20	11	36	541	--	--
Tupelo/gum	598	--	--	153	--	1	12	5	119	309	--	--
Yellow-poplar	57,754	0	0	1,858	--	--	418	1,793	2,614	51,071	--	--
Other hardwoods	3,957	--	--	566	--	--	67	35	919	2,370	--	--
Hardwood total	179,635	199	1,122	14,020	43	143	2,295	7,536	16,943	135,946	68	1,320
State total	189,249	199	1,122	15,876	43	143	6,719	7,561	17,425	138,773	68	1,320

(Table 6 continued on next page)

29

(Table 6 continued)

NORTHEASTERN

Species group	Total	State of destination										
		Indiana	Kentucky	Maryland	Missouri	North Carolina	Ohio	Pennsylvania	Virginia	West Virginia	Wisconsin	Other countries
Softwoods												
Eastern redcedar	0	--	--	--	--	0	--	--	--	0	--	--
Hemlock	416	--	--	136	--	--	0	7	40	233	--	--
Loblolly/shortleaf pine	59	--	--	36	--	--	--	1	1	21	--	--
Red pine	2	--	--	2	--	--	--	--	--	--	--	--
White pine	985	--	--	373	--	--	0	7	39	565	--	--
Other pine	1,631	--	--	1,299	--	--	--	3	69	260	--	--
Spruce	170	--	--	8	--	--	--	--	40	121	--	--
Softwood total	3,263	--	--	1,854	--	0	1	19	189	1,200	--	--
Hardwoods												
Ash	1,322	1	0	295	--	5	1	68	80	835	--	37
Aspen/balsam poplar	116	--	--	19	--	--	--	0	--	97	--	--
Basswood	2,634	--	--	493	--	--	0	115	120	1,905	--	--
Beech	1,072	--	--	407	--	--	0	42	183	440	0	--
Yellow birch	574	0	--	251	--	--	1	11	91	220	--	--
Other birch	1,383	--	--	282	--	--	0	15	143	942	--	--
Black cherry	4,806	69	--	936	--	9	3	198	398	3,068	1	123
Black walnut	95	10	0	--	--	6	0	6	0	73	--	0
Elm	224	--	--	83	--	--	--	1	4	135	--	--
Hickory	1,633	4	--	596	--	--	1	76	92	863	2	--
Hard maple	5,510	17	--	993	--	8	5	322	320	3,662	12	171
Soft maple	9,582	6	--	1,531	--	--	5	362	509	6,942	--	227
Red oak group	14,433	15	31	1,911	--	5	14	1,353	623	10,165	25	291
White oak group	9,805	5	0	2,572	20	--	6	828	431	5,609	--	333
Sycamore	371	--	--	105	--	--	0	5	1	259	--	--
Tupelo/gum	298	--	--	--	--	0	--	4	8	140	--	--
Yellow-poplar	20,489	0	--	1,517	--	--	13	827	268	17,863	--	--
Other hardwoods	1,909	--	--	505	--	--	0	18	122	1,264	--	--
Hardwood total	76,255	125	32	12,643	20	34	51	4,252	3,393	54,482	40	1,182
Unit total	79,518	125	32	14,497	20	34	51	4,271	3,583	55,683	40	1,182

SOUTHERN

							State of destiniation					
Species group	Total	Indiana	Kentucky	Maryland	Missouri	North Carolina	Ohio	Pennsyl- vania	Virginia	West Virginia	Wisconsin	Other countries
Softwoods												
Eastern redcedar	0	--	--	--	--	0	--	--	--	--	--	--
Hemlock	262	--	--	--	--	--	1	2	77	183	--	--
Loblolly/shortleaf pine	74	--	--	--	--	--	--	0	4	70	--	--
Red pine	6	--	--	--	--	--	--	--	6	--	--	--
White pine	1,123	--	--	--	--	--	--	2	53	1,068	--	--
Other pine	242	--	--	--	--	--	48	0	153	41	--	--
Spruce	28	--	--	--	--	--	--	--	1	27	--	--
Softwood total	1,734	--	--	--	--	0	49	4	293	1,388	--	--
Hardwoods												
Ash	934	0	0	--	--	--	5	18	309	602	--	--
Aspen/balsam poplar	1	--	--	--	--	--	--	--	--	1	--	--
Basswood	2,197	--	--	0	--	--	21	31	442	1,704	--	--
Yellow birch	1,445	--	0	0	--	--	10	11	460	965	--	--
Other birch	188	0	--	--	--	--	1	3	134	50	--	--
Beech	564	--	--	0	--	--	0	4	282	278	--	--
Black cherry	1,797	4	--	--	--	40	3	65	498	1,187	--	0
Black walnut	179	5	0	--	--	4	--	1	0	169	--	0
Elm	79	--	--	--	--	--	3	0	29	46	--	--
Hickory	1,515	4	0	0	--	1	19	18	798	672	--	0
Hard maple	3,217	6	--	0	--	3	18	83	609	2,496	1	--
Soft maple	6,860	3	0	0	--	--	22	97	1,246	5,492	--	--
Red oak group	14,319	13	36	0	--	3	63	310	2,559	11,317	18	1
White oak group	9,188	4	0	0	14	9	56	166	2,868	6,071	--	0
Sweetgum	3	--	--	--	--	--	--	--	--	3	--	--
Sycamore	132	--	--	--	--	--	1	1	35	95	--	--
Tupelo/gum	218	--	--	--	--	0	2	1	111	105	--	--
Yellow-poplar	26,803	--	0	0	--	--	61	266	2,341	24,134	--	--
Other hardwoods	1,485	--	--	0	--	--	13	5	797	670	--	--
Hardwood total	71,125	41	37	1	14	60	298	1,080	13,516	56,055	22	1
Unit total	72,859	41	37	1	14	60	347	1,084	13,808	57,443	22	1

(Table 6 continued on next page)

31

(Table 6 continued)

NORTHWESTERN

						State of destiniation						
Species group	Total	Indiana	Kentucky	Maryland	Missouri	North Carolina	Ohio	Pennsyl-vania	Virginia	West Virginia	Wisconsin	Other countries
Softwoods												
Hemlock	24	--	--	--	--	--	0	0	--	24	--	--
Loblolly/shortleaf pine	76	--	--	--	--	--	75	0	--	1	--	--
Red pine	780	--	--	0	--	--	743	1	--	36	--	--
Other pine	3,721	--	--	1	--	--	3,556	1	--	162	--	--
Spruce	15	--	--	--	--	--	--	--	--	15	--	--
Softwood total	4,617	--	--	2	--	--	4,374	2	--	238	--	--
Hardwoods												
Ash	670	1	0	66	--	1	65	62	1	459	--	15
Aspen/balsam poplar	214	--	--	45	--	--	8	0	--	161	--	--
Basswood	503	--	--	24	--	--	36	32	0	411	--	--
Beech	260	--	0	20	--	--	45	12	0	184	--	--
Yellow birch	50	--	--	2	--	--	0	2	0	45	--	--
Other birch	62	--	--	7	--	--	2	3	0	50	--	--
Black cherry	1,068	6	--	131	--	17	77	125	17	661	--	34
Black walnut	286	14	191	--	--	6	6	8	0	61	0	0
Elm	321	--	--	24	--	--	37	4	1	256	--	--
Hickory	729	2	0	75	--	1	116	53	1	476	5	--
Hard maple	1,564	--	--	79	--	1	131	195	1	1,142	1	14
Soft maple	2,492	--	0	187	--	--	143	175	3	1,954	--	31
Red oak group	7,098	5	179	159	--	8	423	549	2	5,742	--	29
White oak group	5,598	4	683	131	9	14	430	266	2	4,046	--	13
Sweetgum	0	--	--	--	--	--	--	--	--	0	--	--
Sycamore	233	--	--	21	--	--	19	5	0	188	--	--
Tupelo/gum	82	--	--	7	--	1	9	1	0	64	--	--
Yellow-poplar	10,463	0	0	340	--	--	344	700	6	9,073	--	--
Other hardwoods	563	--	--	60	--	--	54	12	1	436	--	--
Hardwood total	32,256	32	1,053	1,377	9	49	1,946	2,204	35	25,409	6	136
Unit total	36,872	32	1,053	1,379	9	49	6,321	2,206	35	25,648	6	136

All table cells without observations are indicated by -- . Table value of 0 indicates the volume rounds to less

Table 7. -- Industrial roundwood production in thousand cubic feet, by Forest Inventory Unit, county, and species group, West Virginia, 2007

Forest Inventory Unit and county	All species	Softwoods								Hardwoods			
		Eastern redcedar	Hemlock	Loblolly/ shortleaf pine	Red pine	White pine	Other pine	Spruce	Total softwoods	Ash	Aspen/ balsam poplar	Bass-wood	Beech
Northeastern													
Barbour	2,604	--	11	--	--	23	3	5	41	41	9	32	5
Berkeley	393	0	--	0	--	--	0	--	0	16	--	9	--
Braxton	5,517	--	18	1	--	38	9	9	76	89	--	95	65
Grant	4,014	0	4	--	--	3	20	2	29	125	17	402	45
Hampshire	3,823	--	61	9	--	201	480	--	751	48	1	27	6
Hardy	3,408	0	40	2	--	214	158	2	415	74	--	127	1
Harrison	2,442	--	0	--	--	10	1	0	11	83	11	10	18
Jefferson	287	--	--	--	--	--	--	--	--	16	--	7	--
Lewis	3,324	--	21	--	--	19	18	5	64	33	11	29	34
Mineral	1,966	--	25	26	--	--	263	--	313	74	--	70	--
Morgan	1,768	--	--	--	--	63	465	--	529	31	--	6	--
Pendleton	3,649	--	21	--	--	122	132	12	286	50	0	79	21
Pocahontas	7,225	--	38	20	--	193	35	72	358	201	42	771	130
Preston	7,496	--	13	--	2	16	--	2	33	89	6	151	124
Randolph	11,176	--	33	--	--	30	3	16	82	115	--	249	326
Taylor	872	--	--	--	--	--	--	--	--	20	--	7	1
Tucker	6,252	--	85	--	--	22	2	33	142	104	0	163	140
Upshur	5,619	--	19	--	--	18	18	4	58	37	--	43	35
Webster	7,682	--	28	1	--	12	24	9	74	75	19	354	123
Unit total	79,518	0	416	59	2	985	1,631	170	3,263	1,322	116	2,634	1,072
Southern													
Boone	2,984	--	3	--	--	3	1	--	6	6	--	115	34
Clay	2,750	--	14	1	--	10	9	6	40	33	--	107	21
Fayette	11,692	--	56	3	--	43	7	5	114	50	--	415	293
Greenbrier	13,025	0	39	9	--	57	23	5	133	242	--	186	381
Kanawha	4,886	--	6	--	--	7	54	4	71	120	--	206	44
Logan	1,119	--	--	1	--	0	2	--	3	8	--	50	2
McDowell	3,786	--	1	17	--	160	7	--	185	39	--	71	58
Mercer	6,073	--	10	28	6	384	23	0	450	67	--	161	219
Mingo	1,259	--	0	--	--	0	0	--	1	11	--	38	3
Monroe	2,473	--	--	--	--	97	75	--	172	50	--	66	20
Nicholas	8,518	--	99	1	--	21	8	7	137	75	--	375	219
Raleigh	5,862	--	30	--	--	16	--	1	46	88	1	185	75
Summers	3,616	--	2	--	--	89	34	--	125	95	--	111	17
Wyoming	4,815	--	2	14	--	235	--	--	251	49	--	110	60
Unit total	72,859	0	262	74	6	1,123	242	28	1,734	934	1	2,197	1,445

(Table 7 continued on the next page)

(Table 7 continued)

Northwestern

County	Total											
Brooke	120	—	—	—	—	0	0	0	1	—	—	—
Cabell	1,284	—	—	—	—	—	134	134	31	—	6	2
Calhoun	1,877	—	6	0	4	6	9	26	21	1	29	15
Doddridge	2,072	—	—	—	—	10	4	14	39	56	17	19
Gilmer	1,915	—	6	6	4	5	12	27	25	—	44	64
Hancock	16	—	—	—	—	—	—	—	—	—	—	—
Jackson	1,659	—	—	16	—	—	314	331	36	1	16	7
Lincoln	1,554	—	—	—	—	0	—	0	15	—	21	4
Marion	3,042	—	—	—	—	0	—	0	70	80	55	14
Marshall	497	—	—	—	—	—	—	—	25	8	12	3
Mason	1,281	—	—	7	—	—	207	214	30	2	7	0
Monongalia	4,144	—	0	—	—	—	—	0	101	—	66	28
Ohio	192	—	—	—	—	1	—	1	3	—	—	2
Pleasants	146	—	—	—	—	1	0	1	3	5	3	0
Putnam	1,550	—	—	—	—	20	295	316	47	—	18	15
Ritchie	4,162	—	—	12	—	526	849	1,387	49	12	62	37
Roane	1,970	—	6	—	4	5	6	22	50	5	25	12
Tyler	675	—	—	—	—	—	37	37	12	4	10	6
Wayne	2,427	—	6	0	4	3	24	37	18	—	20	1
Wetzel	2,371	—	—	—	—	0	0	1	58	14	65	17
Wirt	2,879	—	—	40	—	201	1,508	1,749	20	—	10	11
Wood	1,039	—	—	—	—	—	320	320	18	26	16	3
Unit total	36,872	—	24	76	15	780	3,721	4,617	670	214	503	260
State total	189,249	0	703	209	213	2,887	5,594	9,614	2,926	331	5,334	2,778

34

Forest Inventory Unit and county	Yellow birch	Other birch	Black cherry	Black walnut	Elm	Hickory	Hard maple	Soft maple	Red oak group	White oak group	Sweet-gum	Syca-more	Tupelo/gum	Yellow-poplar	Other hardwoods	Total hardwoods
Northeastern																
Barbour	1	18	165	--	4	31	283	397	350	200	--	1	10	963	53	2,563
Berkeley	--	--	60	4	0	7	29	3	125	57	--	--	--	81	1	393
Braxton	19	46	38	15	13	191	261	292	1,193	748	--	72	11	2,167	126	5,442
Grant	10	23	339	7	34	95	580	383	921	626	--	1	33	203	141	3,985
Hampshire	2	9	109	10	15	127	66	130	889	1,310	--	16	39	244	24	3,072
Hardy	1	15	105	12	3	75	172	169	944	1,008	--	10	41	207	30	2,993
Harrison	16	--	108	2	33	71	133	228	261	126	--	131	13	1,125	62	2,431
Jefferson	--	--	59	3	--	4	29	1	84	29	--	2	--	51	2	287
Lewis	4	14	30	4	8	143	131	290	591	333	--	12	17	1,514	61	3,261
Mineral	--	1	140	4	7	90	210	83	391	414	--	--	7	135	27	1,652
Morgan	3	2	60	3	2	24	49	67	387	432	--	23	12	126	15	1,239
Pendleton	12	50	270	4	2	74	344	237	1,159	699	--	3	7	292	61	3,363
Pocahontas	84	313	446	12	19	100	549	1,371	1,342	629	--	--	3	655	200	6,867
Preston	22	93	646	0	21	141	495	1,064	1,651	608	--	8	24	2,175	144	7,463
Randolph	166	429	1,172	4	10	152	993	2,464	1,116	875	--	1	22	2,570	433	11,094
Taylor	--	1	36	1	1	14	58	146	180	66	--	2	3	326	11	872
Tucker	168	101	627	--	37	71	384	743	897	488	--	2	20	2,000	165	6,110
Upshur	26	123	108	5	3	113	274	749	951	474	--	82	18	2,408	110	5,561
Webster	39	145	290	4	12	108	468	765	1,004	685	--	6	19	3,247	244	7,608
Unit total	574	1,383	4,806	95	224	1,633	5,510	9,582	14,433	9,805	--	371	298	20,489	1,909	76,255
Southern																
Boone	12	44	73	3	13	80	120	208	587	581	--	56	15	968	62	2,978
Clay	2	36	20	6	7	63	126	256	624	365	--	2	13	961	68	2,710
Fayette	4	71	212	29	5	315	544	1,134	2,352	1,809	--	21	48	4,088	188	11,579
Greenbrier	115	135	664	30	12	443	562	1,363	2,505	2,184	--	12	39	3,467	553	12,892
Kanawha	3	10	88	6	17	119	279	429	1,220	740	--	10	13	1,424	87	4,815
Logan	0	6	5	3	1	12	21	32	153	61	--	0	2	747	12	1,116
McDowell	2	5	54	14	0	38	59	255	429	219	--	1	1	2,350	7	3,601
Mercer	--	19	154	34	1	76	191	821	1,133	438	--	--	6	2,255	49	5,623
Mingo	2	2	17	7	0	13	33	46	224	111	0	0	1	744	7	1,258
Monroe	--	28	57	1	12	65	137	123	666	480	--	--	2	542	52	2,301
Nicholas	46	177	133	18	4	152	392	1,095	995	804	3	28	59	3,617	188	8,381
Raleigh	2	22	155	10	0	59	332	540	1,364	557	--	0	8	2,310	106	5,816
Summers	--	3	86	6	5	49	268	239	1,265	520	--	--	8	765	55	3,491
Wyoming	1	9	78	13	1	31	153	319	801	320	--	1	2	2,565	51	4,564
Unit total	188	564	1,797	179	79	1,515	3,217	6,860	14,319	9,188	3	132	218	26,803	1,485	71,125

(Table 7 continued on the next page)

35

(Table 7 continued)

Northwestern

County															Total
Brooke	--	--	24	0	5	0	20	3	30	15	1	0	17	4	120
Cabell	2	0	13	76	2	9	66	49	232	416	3	1	237	5	1,150
Calhoun	3	2	8	7	3	81	75	82	589	394	16	2	515	9	1,851
Doddridge	0	0	33	2	3	46	102	256	296	181	3	12	927	67	2,057
Gilmer	4	5	11	7	13	106	85	141	430	323	17	2	580	30	1,887
Hancock	--	--	7	--	0	2	1	5	2	1	--	--	--	--	16
Jackson	1	1	22	3	13	34	80	88	425	300	3	6	274	20	1,329
Lincoln	4	1	8	67	0	22	24	57	374	514	1	1	441	2	1,554
Marion	4	2	213	8	17	58	179	377	599	331	37	4	919	74	3,042
Marshall	--	1	59	8	54	8	39	58	68	23	10	0	105	18	497
Mason	2	0	15	1	4	9	42	43	204	169	2	0	529	7	1,066
Monongalia	6	22	415	7	45	59	221	410	715	411	17	5	1,578	38	4,144
Ohio	--	--	9	0	72	--	22	1	6	--	14	--	5	57	191
Pleasants	3	--	0	0	2	3	9	5	43	24	3	0	40	4	145
Putnam	--	1	12	1	13	19	52	56	305	287	1	10	348	49	1,234
Ritchie	3	11	60	6	15	89	109	240	772	495	26	17	729	42	2,775
Roane	5	3	42	4	4	75	112	130	434	352	24	3	658	11	1,949
Tyler	0	1	20	6	3	12	34	49	91	65	2	2	313	8	638
Wayne	4	2	18	69	1	17	44	125	590	670	0	2	804	4	2,391
Wetzel	4	9	46	3	38	38	158	164	435	252	30	5	961	71	2,370
Wirt	3	1	12	2	8	32	49	73	281	240	11	1	363	13	1,130
Wood	2	0	22	7	8	11	43	80	179	135	8	8	121	32	719
Unit total	50	62	1,068	286	321	729	1,564	2,492	7,098	5,598	233	82	10,463	563	32,256
State total	812	2,010	7,672	560	624	3,877	10,290	18,934	35,851	24,591	735	598	57,754	3,957	179,635

All table cells without observations are indicated by -- Table value of 0 indicates the volume rounds to less

Table 8.-- Industrial roundwood production by Forest Inventory Unit, species group, and product, West Virginia, 2007

ALL UNITS

Species group	All products MCF[a]	Saw logs MBF[b]	Saw logs MCF[a]	Veneer logs MBF[b]	Veneer logs MCF[a]	Pulp and composite products Cords[c]	Pulp and composite products MCF[a]	Cooperage[c] Cords[c]	Cooperage[c] MCF[b]	Handles Pieces	Handles MCF[a]	Posts/fencing[d] M pieces[d]	Posts/fencing MCF[a]	Cabin logs MCF[a]	Mine timbers MCF[a]
Softwoods															
Eastern redcedar	0	--	--	0	0	--	--	--	--	--	--	0	0	--	--
Hemlock	703	710	123	--	--	2,909	247	--	--	--	--	392	302	16	14
Loblolly/shortleaf pine	209	130	23	--	--	2,055	175	--	--	--	--	15	12	--	--
Red pine	8	32	6	--	--	28	2	--	--	--	--	--	--	--	--
White pine	2,887	767	133	--	--	22,576	1,919	--	--	--	--	642	494	22	320
Other pine	5,594	1,340	233	--	--	59,759	5,080	--	--	--	--	350	270	--	12
Spruce	213	14	2	--	--	577	49	--	--	--	--	209	161	--	--
Softwood total	9,614	2,993	520	0	0	87,903	7,472	--	--	--	--	1,609	1,239	38	345
Hardwoods															
Ash	2,926	12,531	2,059	65	9	8,659	736	--	--	731	118	--	--	--	3
Aspen/balsam poplar	331	38	6	259	35	3,399	289	--	--	--	--	--	--	--	--
Basswood	5,334	14,227	2,338	824	113	33,718	2,866	--	--	--	--	--	--	--	17
Beech	2,778	5,246	862	2	0	22,320	1,897	--	--	--	--	--	--	--	19
Yellow birch	812	1,311	215	810	111	5,708	485	--	--	--	--	--	--	--	0
Other birch	2,010	1,784	293	--	--	20,195	1,717	--	--	--	--	--	--	--	--
Black cherry	7,672	32,512	5,342	1,749	239	24,373	2,072	--	--	--	--	--	--	--	19
Black walnut	560	2,695	413	150	21	1,483	126	--	--	--	--	--	--	--	--
Elm	624	465	76	--	--	6,435	547	--	--	--	--	--	--	--	0
Hickory	3,877	12,252	2,013	86	12	19,857	1,688	--	--	787	127	6	3	--	37
Hard maple	10,290	48,416	8,245	446	61	22,855	1,943	--	--	--	--	6	3	--	38
Soft maple	18,934	51,564	8,781	--	--	118,301	10,056	--	--	--	--	6	3	--	94
Red oak group	35,851	179,603	30,389	1,824	250	55,417	4,710	--	--	--	--	394	227	--	275
White oak group	24,591	106,609	18,038	205	28	71,611	6,087	488	80	--	--	143	83	--	275
Sweetgum	3	--	--	--	--	38	3	--	--	--	--	--	--	--	--
Sycamore	735	909	149	--	--	6,854	583	--	--	--	--	5	3	--	0
Tupelo/gum	598	406	67	6	1	6,241	531	--	--	--	--	--	--	--	--
Yellow-poplar	57,754	146,557	24,079	94,152	12,880	232,245	19,741	--	--	--	--	1,413	814	3	237
Other hardwoods	3,957	3,266	537	--	--	36,593	3,110	--	--	--	--	537	309	--	1
Hardwood total	179,635	620,391	103,902	100,579	13,760	696,302	59,186	488	80	1,518	246	2,503	1,442	3	1,016
State total	189,249	623,384	104,422	100,579	13,760	784,205	66,657	488	80	1,518	246	4,112	2,681	41	1,361

(Table 8 continued on next page)

(Table 8 continued)

NORTHEASTERN

Species group	All products MCF[a]	Saw logs MBF[b]	Saw logs MCF[a]	Veneer logs MBF[b]	Veneer logs MCF[a]	Pulp and composite products Cords[c]	Pulp and composite products MCF[a]	Cooperage Cords[c]	Cooperage MCF[a]	Handles Pieces	Handles MCF[a]	Posts/fencing M pieces[d]	Posts/fencing MCF[a]	Cabin logs MCF[a]	Mine timbers MCF[a]
Softwoods															
Eastern redcedar	0	--	--	0	0	--	--	--	--	--	--	0	0	--	--
Hemlock	416	43	7	--	--	2,065	176	--	--	--	--	303	233	--	--
Loblolly/shortleaf pine	59	65	11	--	--	438	37	--	--	--	--	13	10	--	--
Red pine	2	--	--	--	--	28	2	--	--	--	--	--	--	--	--
White pine	985	684	119	--	--	4,958	421	--	--	--	--	569	438	7	--
Other pine	1,631	482	84	--	--	15,493	1,317	--	--	--	--	299	230	--	--
Spruce	170	--	--	--	--	570	48	--	--	--	--	157	121	--	--
Softwood total	3,263	1,274	221	0	0	23,552	2,002	--	--	--	--	1,342	1,033	7	--
Hardwoods															
Ash	1,322	5,360	881	46	6	3,796	323	--	--	690	112	--	--	--	0
Aspen/balsam poplar	116	30	5	109	15	1,129	96	--	--	--	--	--	--	--	--
Basswood	2,634	5,040	828	332	45	20,708	1,760	--	--	--	--	--	--	--	0
Beech	1,072	2,921	480	2	0	6,948	591	--	--	--	--	--	--	--	1
Yellow birch	574	1,160	191	310	42	4,010	341	--	--	--	--	--	--	--	0
Other birch	1,383	1,247	205	--	--	13,859	1,178	--	--	--	--	--	--	--	--
Black cherry	4,806	21,184	3,480	1,110	152	13,589	1,155	--	--	--	--	--	--	--	19
Black walnut	95	543	83	55	8	46	4	--	--	--	--	--	--	--	--
Elm	224	258	42	--	--	2,130	181	--	--	--	--	--	--	--	0
Hickory	1,633	5,087	836	17	2	7,987	679	--	--	690	112	--	--	--	4
Hard maple	5,510	25,210	4,293	350	48	13,554	1,152	--	--	--	--	6	3	--	13
Soft maple	9,582	27,148	4,623	--	--	58,162	4,944	--	--	--	--	6	3	--	12
Red oak group	14,433	71,435	12,087	875	120	23,681	2,013	--	--	--	--	353	203	--	11
White oak group	9,805	40,790	6,902	15	2	32,872	2,794	126	21	--	--	143	83	--	3
Sycamore	371	306	50	--	--	3,733	317	--	--	--	--	5	3	--	0
Tupelo/gum	298	244	40	1	0	3,036	258	--	--	--	--	--	--	--	--
Yellow-poplar	20,489	59,922	9,845	38,731	5,298	54,013	4,591	--	--	--	--	1,271	732	--	22
Other hardwoods	1,909	1,566	257	--	--	16,018	1,362	--	--	--	--	502	289	--	1
Hardwood total	76,255	269,454	45,129	41,953	5,739	279,270	23,738	126	21	1,380	224	2,285	1,316	--	88
Unit total	79,518	270,728	45,351	41,953	5,739	302,823	25,740	126	21	1,380	224	3,627	2,349	7	88

Species group	All products MCF[a]	Saw logs MBF[b]	Saw logs MCF[a]	Veneer logs MBF[b]	Veneer logs MCF[a]	Pulp and composite products Cords[c]	Pulp and composite products MCF[a]	Cooperage Cords[c]	Cooperage MCF[a]	Handles Pieces	Handles MCF[a]	Posts/fencing M pieces[d]	Posts/fencing MCF[a]	Cabin logs MCF[a]	Mine timbers MCF[a]
Softwoods															
Eastern redcedar	0	--	--	0	0	--	--	--	--	--	--	--	--	--	--
Hemlock	262	665	116	--	--	844	72	--	--	--	--	58	45	16	14
Loblolly/shortleaf pine	74	63	11	--	--	721	61	--	--	--	--	2	2	--	--
Red pine	6	32	6	--	--	--	--	--	--	--	--	--	--	--	--
White pine	1,123	72	13	--	--	8,799	748	--	--	--	--	47	36	7	320
Other pine	242	782	136	--	--	965	82	--	--	--	--	30	23	1	1
Spruce	28	14	2	--	--	7	1	--	--	--	--	32	25	--	--
Softwood total	**1,734**	**1,628**	**283**	**0**	**0**	**11,335**	**964**	**--**	**--**	**--**	**--**	**169**	**130**	**23**	**335**
Hardwoods															
Ash	934	3,773	620	5	1	3,646	310	--	--	--	--	--	--	--	3
Aspen/balsam poplar	1	--	--	7	1	2	0	--	--	--	--	--	--	--	--
Basswood	2,197	7,340	1,206	399	55	10,816	919	--	--	--	--	--	--	--	17
Beech	1,445	1,098	180	--	--	14,680	1,248	--	--	--	--	--	--	--	17
Yellow birch	188	134	22	176	24	1,669	142	--	--	--	--	--	--	--	--
Other birch	564	387	64	--	--	5,892	501	--	--	--	--	--	--	--	--
Black cherry	1,797	5,951	978	373	51	9,042	769	--	--	--	--	--	--	--	--
Black walnut	179	369	56	33	5	1,389	118	--	--	--	--	--	--	--	--
Elm	79	63	10	--	--	803	68	--	--	--	--	--	--	--	--
Hickory	1,515	3,834	630	33	5	9,973	848	--	--	--	--	--	--	--	33
Hard maple	3,217	14,859	2,531	80	11	7,646	650	--	--	--	--	--	--	--	25
Soft maple	6,860	15,159	2,582	--	--	49,769	4,230	--	--	--	--	--	--	--	48
Red oak group	14,319	69,401	11,743	701	96	27,736	2,358	--	--	--	--	14	8	--	115
White oak group	9,188	36,343	6,149	75	10	34,112	2,900	104	17	--	--	--	--	--	112
Sweetgum	3	--	--	--	--	38	3	--	--	--	--	--	--	--	--
Sycamore	132	146	24	--	--	1,269	108	--	--	--	--	--	--	--	--
Tupelo/gum	218	111	18	1	0	2,351	200	--	--	--	--	--	--	--	--
Yellow-poplar	26,803	53,246	8,748	32,477	4,443	158,741	13,493	--	--	--	--	71	41	3	74
Other hardwoods	1,485	1,410	232	--	--	14,640	1,244	--	--	--	--	16	9	--	--
Hardwood total	**71,125**	**213,621**	**35,792**	**34,360**	**4,701**	**354,212**	**30,108**	**104**	**17**	**--**	**--**	**101**	**58**	**3**	**446**
Unit total	**72,859**	**215,250**	**36,075**	**34,360**	**4,701**	**365,548**	**31,072**	**104**	**17**	**--**	**--**	**270**	**188**	**26**	**780**

(Table 8 continued on next page)

39

(Table 8 continued)

NORTHWESTERN

Species group	All products MCF[a]	Saw logs MBF[b]	Saw logs MCF[a]	Veneer logs MBF[b]	Veneer logs MCF[a]	Pulp and composite products Cords[c]	Pulp and composite products MCF[a]	Cooperage Cords[c]	Cooperage MCF[a]	Handles Pieces	Handles MCF[a]	Posts/fencing M pieces[d]	Posts/fencing MCF[a]	Cabin logs MCF[a]	Mine timbers MCF[a]
Softwoods															
Hemlock	24	2	0	--	--	--	--	--	--	--	--	31	24	--	--
Loblolly/shortleaf pine	76	2	0	--	--	896	76	--	--	--	--	--	--	--	--
White pine	780	11	2	--	--	8,818	750	--	--	--	--	26	20	9	--
Other pine	3,721	76	13	--	--	43,301	3,681	--	--	--	--	21	16	--	10
Spruce	15	--	--	--	--	--	--	--	--	--	--	20	15	--	--
Softwood total	4,617	91	16	--	--	53,015	4,506	--	--	--	--	98	75	9	10
Hardwoods															
Ash	670	3,399	558	13	2	1,217	103	--	--	41	7	--	--	--	--
Aspen/balsam poplar	214	8	1	143	19	2,268	193	--	--	--	--	--	--	--	--
Basswood	503	1,847	304	93	13	2,194	187	--	--	--	--	--	--	--	--
Beech	260	1,226	201	--	--	692	59	--	--	--	--	--	--	--	--
Yellow birch	50	17	3	325	44	29	2	--	--	--	--	--	--	--	--
Other birch	62	150	25	--	--	444	38	--	--	--	--	--	--	--	--
Black cherry	1,068	5,378	884	266	36	1,742	148	--	--	--	--	--	--	--	--
Black walnut	286	1,783	273	61	9	48	4	--	--	--	--	--	--	--	--
Elm	321	145	24	--	--	3,502	298	--	--	--	--	--	--	--	--
Hickory	729	3,331	547	36	5	1,896	161	--	--	97	16	--	--	--	34
Hard maple	1,564	8,346	1,421	16	2	1,655	141	--	--	--	--	--	--	--	--
Soft maple	2,492	9,256	1,576	--	--	10,370	881	--	--	--	--	--	--	--	--
Red oak group	7,098	38,767	6,559	248	34	4,001	340	--	--	--	--	27	16	--	149
White oak group	5,598	29,476	4,987	116	16	4,627	393	258	43	--	--	--	--	--	159
Sweetgum	0	--	--	--	--	0	0	--	--	--	--	--	--	--	--
Sycamore	233	458	75	--	--	1,852	157	--	--	--	--	--	--	--	--
Tupelo/gum	82	50	8	5	1	855	73	--	--	--	--	--	--	--	--
Yellow-poplar	10,463	33,389	5,486	22,944	3,139	19,491	1,657	--	--	--	--	71	41	--	140
Other hardwoods	563	290	48	--	--	5,935	505	--	--	--	--	19	11	--	--
Hardwood total	32,256	137,316	22,981	24,266	3,320	62,819	5,340	258	43	138	22	117	68	--	483
Unit total	36,872	137,407	22,997	24,266	3,320	115,834	9,846	258	43	138	22	215	143	9	493

[a] Thousand cubic feet.
[b] Thousand board feet, International 1/4-inch rule.
[c] Standard cords are 128 cubic feet consisting of 85 cubic feet of wood and 43 cubic feet of bark and air space.
[d] Thousand pieces.
All table cells without observations are indicated by -- . Table value of 0 indicates the volume rounds to less than 1/2 unit of measure.

Table 9. -- Saw log receipts and production in thousand board feet, International 1/4-inch rule, by Forest Inventory Unit and species group, West Virginia, 2000 and 2007

ALL UNITS

Species group	Receipts			Production		
	2000[a]	2007	Percent change	2000[a]	2007	Percent change
Softwood						
Eastern redcedar	--	--	--	--	--	--
Hemlock	--	621	--	--	710	--
Loblolly/shortleaf pine	--	150	--	--	130	--
Red pine	--	--	--	--	32	--
White pine	--	863	--	--	767	--
Other pine	--	364	--	--	1,340	--
Spruce	--	14	--	--	14	--
Softwood total	3,462	2,012	-42%	5,144	2,993	-42%
Hardwood						
Ash	12,048	12,888	7%	12,341	12,531	2%
Aspen/balsam poplar	--	54	--	--	38	--
Basswood	18,608	15,354	-17%	18,597	14,227	-23%
Beech	4,447	5,247	18%	4,531	5,246	16%
Yellow birch	--	1,608	--	1,504	1,311	-13%
Other birch	2,008	1,972	-2%	--	1,784	--
Black cherry	17,927	34,291	91%	18,811	32,512	73%
Black walnut	1,595	1,550	-3%	1,585	2,695	70%
Elm	609	477	-22%	589	465	-21%
Hickory	13,510	12,184	-10%	13,557	12,252	-10%
Hard maple	32,835	50,384	53%	33,573	48,416	44%
Soft maple	24,406	52,330	114%	25,027	51,564	106%
Red oak group	155,076	182,934	18%	158,337	179,603	13%
White oak group	90,681	104,715	15%	87,866	106,609	21%
Sycamore	--	924	--	--	909	--
Tupelo/gum	821	460	-44%	841	406	-52%
Yellow-poplar	112,585	163,110	45%	118,009	146,557	24%
Other hardwoods	6,959	2,763	-60%	8,698	3,266	-62%
Hardwood total	494,115	643,245	30%	503,866	620,391	23%
Unknown species	294,508	--	--	294,508	--	--
All species	792,085	645,257	-19%	803,518	623,384	-22%

Detailed saw log receipts are not available for softwood species.

[a] Table cells without observations are indicated by -- . Table value of 0 indicates the volume rounds to less than 1 thousand board feet. Columns and rows may not add to their totals due to rounding.

Table 10.-- Wood material harvested for industrial roundwood in thousand cubic feet, by Forest Inventory Unit, source of material, and species group, West Virginia, 2007[a]

ALL UNITS

	Source of material													
	Growing stock				Non-growing stock									
	Used for products				Used for products									
Species group	Sawtimber	Pole-timber	Logging residue (not used)	Total growing stock	Limbwood	Saplings	Cull trees	Dead trees	Nonforest trees	Logging slash (not used)	Total non-growing stock	Total used	Total not used	Total harvested
Softwoods														
Eastern redcedar	0.1	0.1	0.0	0.2	--	0.1	0.0	0.0	--	0.1	0.2	0.3	0.1	0.4
Hemlock	267.1	330.5	18.9	616.5	2.4	79.2	7.6	16.1	--	343.4	448.5	702.8	362.2	1,065.0
Loblolly/shortleaf pine	70.2	131.6	4.4	206.2	--	3.1	3.4	0.6	--	84.6	91.6	208.9	89.0	297.9
Red pine	6.2	1.7	0.6	8.5	--	--	0.1	--	--	7.9	7.9	7.9	8.5	16.4
White pine	795.5	1,808.4	63.7	2,667.7	53.9	129.6	73.7	26.3	--	924.4	1,208.0	2,887.5	988.2	3,875.6
Other pine	1,607.1	3,800.3	83.7	5,491.2	2.0	70.7	99.0	14.4	--	1,896.4	2,082.5	5,593.5	1,980.1	7,573.6
Spruce	48.0	112.2	0.8	161.0	--	42.3	1.6	8.6	--	66.0	118.4	212.6	66.8	279.4
Softwood total	2,794.2	6,184.9	172.2	9,151.3	58.2	324.9	185.3	66.0	--	3,322.6	3,957.1	9,613.6	3,494.8	13,108.4
Hardwoods														
Ash	2,498.1	63.1	725.8	3,287.0	206.9	0.6	132.2	24.8	--	1,347.9	1,712.3	2,925.6	2,073.7	4,999.3
Aspen/balsam poplar	219.7	12.6	18.0	250.3	49.9	0.0	46.4	1.9	--	11.9	110.2	330.5	29.9	360.5
Basswood	4,112.1	126.5	818.3	5,056.9	587.1	0.3	466.8	40.9	--	1,575.8	2,670.9	5,333.8	2,394.1	7,727.9
Beech	1,998.0	86.5	328.4	2,413.0	363.2	0.1	309.7	20.4	--	595.8	1,289.3	2,778.0	924.3	3,702.3
Yellow birch	616.6	19.2	98.8	734.5	92.0	--	78.8	5.2	--	155.5	331.4	811.6	254.2	1,065.9
Other birch	1,343.3	67.4	151.9	1,562.6	306.9	--	278.3	13.7	--	224.2	823.1	2,009.6	376.1	2,385.7
Black cherry	6,595.7	104.7	1,695.3	8,395.8	566.9	0.9	338.1	65.3	--	3,508.9	4,480.1	7,671.6	5,204.3	12,875.9
Black walnut	439.1	7.4	38.9	485.4	29.0	0.2	30.9	0.8	52.3	58.9	172.2	559.7	97.9	657.6
Elm	402.0	34.6	42.6	479.2	96.2	0.9	85.6	4.4	--	60.4	247.5	623.7	103.0	726.7
Hickory	3,057.7	122.8	758.1	3,938.6	374.5	0.6	290.8	30.4	--	1,338.4	2,034.7	3,876.8	2,096.5	5,973.3
Hard maple	9,075.7	114.0	2,254.1	11,443.8	717.4	1.2	369.2	12.5	0.4	4,914.1	6,014.8	10,290.4	7,168.1	17,458.5
Soft maple	14,566.2	460.0	2,698.8	17,725.0	2,148.5	0.8	1,694.6	63.8	0.4	5,392.4	9,300.4	18,934.2	8,091.1	27,025.4
Red oak group	31,577.0	403.8	8,678.7	40,659.5	2,044.2	9.8	984.5	804.6	26.8	17,000.1	20,870.1	35,850.7	25,678.8	61,529.5
White oak group	20,724.9	427.1	5,286.7	26,438.7	1,798.3	4.0	1,129.2	497.9	9.7	10,152.9	13,592.0	24,591.2	15,439.6	40,030.8
Sweetgum	2.0	0.1	0.1	2.3	0.6	--	0.5	0.0	--	0.1	1.2	3.2	0.2	3.4
Sycamore	502.1	27.0	66.1	595.2	105.9	0.4	94.1	5.2	0.3	108.4	314.3	735.1	174.5	909.5
Tupelo/gum	393.0	21.2	40.0	454.2	93.9	0.0	85.9	4.0	--	53.9	237.7	598.1	93.8	691.9
Yellow-poplar	48,427.2	1,095.5	9,821.2	59,343.9	4,383.8	33.6	3,350.0	368.1	96.1	16,735.0	24,966.6	57,754.3	26,556.2	84,310.4
Other hardwoods	2,580.2	194.5	276.4	3,051.0	559.0	13.0	545.8	28.2	36.5	414.4	1,596.9	3,957.2	690.7	4,647.9
Hardwood total	149,130.7	3,387.9	33,798.2	186,316.8	14,524.1	66.3	10,311.5	1,992.3	222.5	63,649.0	90,765.6	179,635.3	97,447.1	277,082.4
State total	151,925.0	9,572.8	33,970.3	195,468.1	14,582.3	391.2	10,496.8	2,058.3	222.5	66,971.6	94,722.7	189,248.9	100,941.9	290,190.8

NORTHEASTERN

Source of material

| | Growing stock | | | | Non-growing stock | | | | | | | | | |
| | Used for products | | | | Used for products | | | | | | | | | |
Species group	Sawtimber	Pole-timber	Logging residue (not used)	Total growing stock	Limbwood	Saplings	Cull trees	Dead trees	Nonforest trees	Logging slash (not used)	Total non-growing stock	Total used	Total not used	Total harvested
Softwoods														
Eastern redcedar	0.1	0.1	0.0	0.2	--	0.1	0.0	0.0	--	0.1	0.2	0.3	0.1	0.4
Hemlock	100.6	237.9	2.8	341.3	--	61.2	4.3	12.4	--	131.9	209.7	416.3	134.7	551.0
Loblolly/shortleaf pine	23.1	31.7	1.6	56.4	--	2.7	0.8	0.5	--	28.7	32.7	58.7	30.3	89.1
Red pine	0.6	1.7	0.0	2.3	--	--	0.0	--	--	0.7	0.7	2.4	0.7	3.1
White pine	323.8	512.9	18.2	854.9	--	114.9	9.9	23.3	--	417.5	565.6	984.8	435.7	1,420.5
Other pine	472.3	1,059.8	24.0	1,556.1	--	60.4	26.0	12.2	--	569.5	668.1	1,630.7	593.5	2,224.2
Spruce	37.3	92.7	0.6	130.6	--	31.8	1.4	6.5	--	50.8	90.4	169.6	51.3	220.9
Softwood total	957.7	1,936.8	47.2	2,941.8	--	271.0	42.3	55.0	--	1,199.1	1,567.4	3,262.9	1,246.3	4,509.2
Hardwoods														
Ash	1,120.3	35.6	356.5	1,512.3	89.9	--	65.3	10.6	--	577.8	743.5	1,321.6	934.3	2,255.9
Aspen/balsam poplar	79.2	3.8	7.4	90.4	16.7	--	15.6	0.7	--	6.0	39.0	115.9	13.4	129.3
Basswood	1,924.5	69.2	318.6	2,312.3	335.3	--	285.7	19.2	--	573.6	1,213.9	2,634.0	892.2	3,526.2
Beech	823.1	24.0	164.6	1,011.7	120.6	--	96.1	8.4	--	322.2	547.4	1,072.3	486.8	1,559.1
Yellow birch	435.0	13.5	75.7	524.2	66.1	--	55.4	4.0	--	132.6	258.1	574.1	208.3	782.3
Other birch	925.5	46.2	105.4	1,077.1	210.8	--	191.0	9.5	--	156.3	567.5	1,382.9	261.7	1,644.6
Black cherry	4,179.6	56.4	1,097.6	5,333.7	337.6	--	191.3	41.2	--	2,282.3	2,852.4	4,806.2	3,379.9	8,186.1
Black walnut	78.6	0.2	7.3	86.1	2.2	--	2.9	0.0	--	11.7	27.8	94.8	19.0	113.9
Elm	152.6	7.2	19.4	179.3	32.9	--	29.4	1.6	11.0	31.1	94.9	223.6	50.5	274.2
Hickory	1,295.1	51.6	356.5	1,703.2	150.1	--	123.3	12.4	--	555.8	841.7	1,632.6	912.3	2,544.9
Hard maple	4,834.7	53.6	1,181.4	6,069.6	397.2	0.1	216.3	7.3	0.4	2,562.5	3,183.9	5,509.6	3,743.9	9,253.5
Soft maple	7,451.2	201.7	1,404.9	9,057.8	1,064.9	0.1	832.6	31.3	0.4	2,831.5	4,760.8	9,582.2	4,236.4	13,818.6
Red oak group	12,710.6	126.6	3,452.7	16,289.8	821.9	8.1	420.2	322.0	24.0	6,765.9	8,362.1	14,433.4	10,218.5	24,651.9
White oak group	8,214.2	128.5	2,028.9	10,371.6	751.8	3.3	503.3	193.9	9.7	3,892.6	5,354.7	9,804.7	5,921.5	15,726.3
Sycamore	246.0	13.2	26.9	286.1	56.6	0.1	51.9	2.5	0.3	39.0	150.5	370.7	65.9	436.5
Tupelo/gum	198.3	10.1	21.7	230.1	46.0	--	41.8	2.0	--	31.2	121.0	298.3	52.9	351.2
Yellow-poplar	17,858.3	342.0	3,882.3	22,082.6	1,185.3	29.2	855.2	132.6	86.4	6,777.7	9,066.4	20,489.0	10,660.0	31,149.0
Other hardwoods	1,227.2	112.7	127.9	1,467.8	247.6	11.5	261.5	14.1	34.1	198.2	767.1	1,908.8	326.1	2,234.9
Hardwood total	63,754.0	1,296.0	14,635.6	79,685.6	5,933.4	52.6	4,238.9	813.4	166.4	27,748.0	38,952.6	76,254.6	42,383.6	118,638.2
Unit total	64,711.8	3,232.8	14,682.8	82,627.4	5,933.4	323.6	4,281.2	868.5	166.4	28,947.0	40,520.0	79,517.6	43,629.9	123,147.4

(Table 10 continued on next page)

(Table 10 continued)

SOUTHERN

| Species group | Growing stock | | | | Non-growing stock | | | | | | | Total used | Total not used | Total harvested |
| | Used for products | | Logging residue (not used) | Total growing stock | Used for products | | | | | Logging slash (not used) | Total non-growing stock | | | |
	Sawtimber	Pole-timber			Limbwood	Saplings	Cull trees	Dead trees	Nonforest trees					
Softwoods														
Eastern redcedar	0.0	--	0.0	0.0	--	--	--	--	--	0.0	0.0	0.0	0.0	0.0
Hemlock	161.3	81.2	16.0	258.6	2.4	11.7	3.2	2.4	--	203.9	223.6	262.2	220.0	482.2
Loblolly/shortleaf pine	27.1	44.9	1.9	73.9	--	0.4	1.2	0.1	--	32.7	34.3	73.7	34.5	108.2
Red pine	5.6	--	0.6	6.2	--	--	0.0	--	--	7.2	7.2	5.6	7.7	13.3
White pine	262.5	745.3	35.8	1,043.6	53.9	9.5	49.5	1.9	--	263.5	378.4	1,122.7	299.3	1,422.0
Other pine	161.9	70.9	15.6	248.4	0.2	6.1	1.9	1.2	--	205.5	214.9	242.2	221.0	463.3
Spruce	7.6	12.1	0.3	20.0	--	6.5	0.1	1.3	--	10.6	18.5	27.6	10.9	38.5
Softwood total	625.9	954.5	70.2	1,650.7	56.5	34.1	56.0	6.9	--	723.3	876.9	1,734.0	793.5	2,527.5
Hardwoods														
Ash	782.7	14.1	195.5	992.2	78.0	--	50.9	8.0	--	407.0	544.0	933.7	602.5	1,536.2
Aspen/balsam poplar	1.0	0.0	0.1	1.2	0.0	--	0.0	0.0	--	0.1	0.1	1.1	0.2	1.3
Basswood	1,773.5	46.2	401.2	2,220.9	208.1	--	151.6	17.6	--	801.5	1,178.8	2,197.0	1,202.7	3,399.7
Beech	947.7	59.1	102.1	1,108.9	224.7	--	204.2	9.7	--	142.2	580.7	1,445.4	244.3	1,689.7
Yellow birch	132.9	5.6	15.5	153.9	25.3	--	23.0	1.1	--	18.5	67.8	187.8	33.9	221.7
Other birch	371.1	19.7	37.8	428.5	88.7	--	81.2	3.8	--	51.2	224.9	564.4	89.0	653.4
Black cherry	1,457.3	30.2	326.0	1,813.4	170.4	--	125.1	14.4	--	650.5	960.4	1,797.3	976.5	2,773.9
Black walnut	124.4	4.6	9.3	138.3	21.4	--	20.6	0.7	7.4	10.2	60.4	179.1	19.5	198.6
Elm	52.1	2.7	5.6	60.5	12.2	--	11.1	0.5	--	8.0	31.8	78.6	13.7	92.2
Hickory	1,133.5	52.7	221.8	1,408.0	176.0	--	141.4	11.5	--	425.1	754.0	1,515.1	646.9	2,162.0
Hard maple	2,815.7	40.3	694.0	3,550.0	232.0	--	124.4	4.1	--	1,509.0	1,869.6	3,216.5	2,203.0	5,419.6
Soft maple	5,076.9	194.3	843.6	6,114.8	854.6	--	707.4	26.8	--	1,611.4	3,200.2	6,860.0	2,455.0	9,315.0
Red oak group	12,500.8	162.1	3,374.8	16,037.7	883.4	0.3	458.3	313.4	1.0	6,578.9	8,235.3	14,319.2	9,953.7	24,273.0
White oak group	7,559.3	180.1	1,832.8	9,572.1	758.1	--	516.4	174.6	--	3,477.5	4,926.7	9,188.4	5,310.3	14,498.8
Sweetgum	2.0	0.1	0.1	2.2	0.6	--	0.5	0.0	--	0.1	1.2	3.2	0.2	3.4
Sycamore	89.6	4.2	11.2	105.0	19.5	--	17.5	0.9	--	17.7	55.6	131.8	28.8	160.6
Tupelo/gum	141.4	7.8	13.0	162.3	35.1	--	32.4	1.4	--	15.9	84.8	218.2	28.9	247.1
Yellow-poplar	21,161.4	581.6	3,772.8	25,515.7	2,676.7	1.6	2,205.5	171.0	4.8	6,191.6	11,251.3	26,802.6	9,964.4	36,767.1
Other hardwoods	996.5	50.7	115.8	1,163.0	223.3	0.4	203.1	10.2	1.1	175.1	613.2	1,485.3	290.9	1,776.1
Hardwood total	57,119.6	1,456.0	11,973.1	70,548.7	6,688.2	2.3	5,074.5	769.9	14.2	22,091.5	34,640.7	71,124.8	34,064.6	105,189.4
Unit total	57,745.6	2,410.6	12,043.2	72,199.4	6,744.7	36.5	5,130.5	776.8	14.2	22,814.9	35,517.5	72,858.8	34,858.1	107,716.9

NORTHWESTERN

Source of material

| Species group | Growing stock | | | | Non-growing stock | | | | | | | Total used | Total not used | Total harvested |
| | Used for products | | Logging residue (not used) | Total growing stock | Used for products | | | | | Logging slash (not used) | Total non-growing stock | | | |
	Sawtimber	Pole-timber			Limbwood	Saplings	Cull trees	Dead trees	Nonforest trees					
Softwoods														
Hemlock	5.2	11.4	0.0	16.6	--	6.3	0.1	1.3	--	7.6	15.2	24.2	7.6	31.8
Loblolly/shortleaf pine	20.1	54.9	0.9	75.9	--	--	1.4	--	--	23.2	24.6	76.5	24.1	100.6
White pine	209.2	550.2	9.7	769.1	--	5.2	14.3	1.1	--	243.4	264.0	780.0	253.1	1,033.1
Other pine	972.9	2,669.6	44.2	3,686.7	1.8	4.3	71.1	0.9	--	1,121.4	1,199.5	3,720.6	1,165.6	4,886.2
Spruce	3.1	7.3	--	10.5	--	4.0	0.1	0.8	--	4.6	9.5	15.4	4.6	20.0
Softwood total	1,210.5	3,293.5	54.8	4,558.8	1.8	19.8	87.0	4.0	--	1,400.2	1,512.9	4,616.7	1,455.0	6,071.7
Hardwoods														
Ash	595.2	13.4	173.8	782.4	38.9	0.6	16.0	6.2	--	363.2	424.8	670.3	537.0	1,207.2
Aspen/balsam poplar	139.4	8.8	10.5	158.8	33.1	0.0	30.8	1.2	--	5.8	71.1	213.5	16.3	229.8
Basswood	414.1	11.1	98.5	523.7	43.6	0.3	29.5	4.2	--	200.7	278.3	502.8	299.2	802.0
Beech	227.2	3.4	61.8	292.4	17.9	0.1	9.4	2.3	--	131.4	161.1	260.3	193.2	453.5
Yellow birch	48.7	0.1	7.6	56.4	0.5	--	0.4	0.0	--	4.5	5.5	49.8	12.1	61.8
Other birch	46.8	1.5	8.7	57.0	7.5	--	6.1	0.5	--	16.6	30.7	62.3	25.4	87.7
Black cherry	958.8	18.2	271.7	1,248.7	58.9	0.9	21.6	9.7	--	576.2	667.3	1,068.1	847.8	1,915.9
Black walnut	236.1	2.6	22.4	261.1	5.5	0.2	7.4	0.1	33.9	37.0	84.0	285.8	59.3	345.1
Elm	197.3	24.7	17.5	239.5	51.2	0.9	45.2	2.3	--	21.3	120.8	321.5	38.8	360.3
Hickory	629.1	18.4	179.8	827.4	48.4	0.6	26.1	6.5	--	357.5	439.0	729.1	537.4	1,266.4
Hard maple	1,425.3	20.2	378.7	1,824.2	88.2	1.0	28.5	1.1	--	842.5	961.3	1,564.3	1,221.2	2,785.5
Soft maple	2,038.1	64.0	450.3	2,552.4	229.0	0.7	154.6	5.7	--	949.5	1,339.4	2,492.0	1,399.8	3,891.8
Red oak group	6,365.6	115.2	1,851.2	8,331.9	338.9	1.4	106.1	169.1	1.8	3,655.4	4,272.7	7,098.1	5,506.5	12,604.6
White oak group	4,951.5	118.6	1,425.0	6,495.1	288.5	0.7	109.5	129.4	--	2,782.7	3,310.7	5,598.0	4,207.7	9,805.7
Sweetgum	0.0	0.0	0.0	0.0	0.0	--	0.0	0.0	--	0.0	0.0	0.0	0.0	0.0
Sycamore	166.5	9.6	28.0	204.1	29.8	0.2	24.8	1.8	--	51.8	108.3	232.6	79.8	312.4
Tupelo/gum	53.3	3.3	5.3	61.8	12.8	0.0	11.7	0.5	--	6.8	31.9	81.6	12.1	93.6
Yellow-poplar	9,407.5	172.0	2,166.1	11,745.6	521.8	2.8	289.3	64.5	4.8	3,765.6	4,648.8	10,462.7	5,931.7	16,394.4
Other hardwoods	356.5	31.1	32.7	420.3	88.1	1.1	81.2	3.9	1.3	41.1	216.6	563.1	73.8	636.9
Hardwood total	28,257.1	635.9	7,189.5	36,082.4	1,902.5	11.4	998.1	409.0	41.9	13,809.4	17,172.3	32,255.8	20,998.9	53,254.8
Unit total	29,467.6	3,929.4	7,244.3	40,641.3	1,904.3	31.2	1,085.1	413.0	41.9	15,209.7	18,685.2	36,872.5	22,454.0	59,326.5

a Based on factors obtained from regional utilization studies.

All table cells without observations are indicated by – –. Table value of 0.0 indicates the volume rounds to less than 0.1 thousand cubic feet. Columns and rows may not add to their totals due to rounding.

Table 11.-- Growing-stock removals from timberland for industrial roundwood in thousand cubic feet, by Forest Inventory Unit, county, and species group, West Virginia, 2007

Forest Inventory Unit and county	All species	Softwoods								Hardwoods			
		Eastern redcedar	Hemlock	Loblolly/ shortleaf pine	Red pine	White pine	Other pine	Spruce	Total softwoods	Ash	Aspen/ balsam poplar	Bass-wood	Beech
Northeastern													
Barbour	2,896	--	7	--	--	16	2	3	28	51	8	32	6
Berkeley	476	0	--	0	--	--	0	0	0	19	--	11	--
Braxton	5,962	--	13	1	--	28	7	6	54	104	--	91	61
Grant	3,953	0	3	--	--	2	15	1	22	130	12	318	35
Hampshire	3,759	--	61	9	--	205	477	--	752	49	1	26	4
Hardy	3,565	0	39	1	--	212	154	1	407	85	--	121	1
Harrison	2,556	--	0	--	--	7	1	0	8	96	8	12	17
Jefferson	348	--	--	--	--	--	--	--	0	20	--	9	--
Lewis	3,734	--	14	--	--	13	13	4	44	41	9	36	42
Mineral	1,874	--	25	26	--	--	261	--	311	67	--	59	--
Morgan	1,653	--	--	--	--	63	468	--	531	28	--	7	--
Pendleton	4,062	--	19	--	--	88	94	11	211	58	0	81	21
Pocahontas	7,327	--	34	19	--	148	32	59	291	256	32	620	134
Preston	8,132	--	9	--	2	15	--	1	28	106	5	154	119
Randolph	10,868	--	23	--	--	23	2	11	59	123	--	216	281
Taylor	970	--	--	--	--	--	--	--	0	24	--	7	1
Tucker	6,473	--	62	--	--	15	2	25	103	115	0	164	119
Upshur	5,905	--	13	--	--	13	13	3	41	46	--	47	40
Webster	8,115	--	19	1	--	8	16	6	50	94	16	299	131
Unit total	82,627	0	341	56	2	855	1,556	131	2,942	1,512	90	2,312	1,012
Southern													
Boone	3,264	--	2	--	--	2	1	--	5	8	--	114	38
Clay	3,036	--	10	1	--	7	6	4	28	41	--	103	26
Fayette	11,277	--	57	3	--	40	6	3	109	55	--	440	224
Greenbrier	11,204	0	40	10	--	56	23	4	133	202	--	168	276
Kanawha	5,609	--	4	--	--	5	53	3	65	147	--	215	48
Logan	1,280	--	--	--	--	0	3	--	3	10	--	50	2
McDowell	3,653	--	2	17	--	159	7	--	185	46	--	83	41
Mercer	5,825	--	10	28	--	366	25	0	435	74	--	162	153
Mingo	1,489	--	0	--	--	0	0	--	1	14	--	44	3
Monroe	2,660	--	--	--	--	82	81	--	163	56	--	77	16
Nicholas	7,807	--	99	1	--	18	6	5	129	76	--	314	170
Raleigh	6,216	--	32	--	--	15	--	1	48	96	1	197	55
Summers	4,103	--	2	--	--	74	37	--	113	106	--	129	13
Wyoming	4,777	--	2	14	--	218	--	--	234	60	--	126	43
Unit total	72,199	0	259	74	6	1,044	248	20	1,651	992	1	2,221	1,109

Northwestern

County												
Brooke	138	--	--	--	0	--	--	0	1	--	--	--
Cabell	1,464	--	--	--	--	133	--	133	37	--	8	2
Calhoun	2,241	--	4	--	4	8	3	20	27	1	33	18
Doddridge	2,121	--	--	--	11	3	--	15	46	41	16	16
Gilmer	2,182	--	4	--	4	10	3	20	31	--	49	80
Hancock	19	--	--	--	--	--	--	0	--	--	--	--
Jackson	1,804	--	--	16	--	312	--	328	42	1	18	7
Lincoln	1,854	--	--	--	0	--	--	0	18	--	26	4
Marion	3,283	--	--	--	0	--	--	0	77	58	55	16
Marshall	513	--	--	--	--	--	--	0	28	5	11	3
Mason	1,455	--	--	7	--	206	--	213	37	2	8	0
Monongalia	4,621	--	0	--	--	--	--	0	107	--	69	34
Ohio	157	--	--	--	1	--	--	1	3	--	--	3
Pleasants	171	--	--	--	1	0	--	1	4	4	3	0
Putnam	1,654	--	--	--	20	293	--	313	54	--	17	14
Ritchie	4,430	--	--	--	522	843	--	1,377	56	9	58	36
Roane	2,330	--	4	--	4	5	3	16	62	5	29	15
Tyler	762	--	--	--	--	37	--	37	14	3	10	7
Wayne	2,695	--	4	--	2	22	3	31	23	--	25	1
Wetzel	2,626	--	--	--	0	0	--	1	70	11	58	21
Wirt	3,001	--	--	40	199	1,497	--	1,736	24	--	13	12
Wood	1,121	--	--	--	--	317	--	317	22	19	17	4
Unit total	40,641	--	17	76	769	3,687	10	4,559	782	159	524	292
State total	195,468	0	617	206	2,668	5,491	161	9,151	3,287	250	5,057	2,413

(Table 11 continued on the next page)

(Table 11 continued)

Forest Inventory Unit and county	Yellow birch	Other birch	Black cherry	Black walnut	Elm	Hickory	Hard maple	Soft maple	Red oak group	White oak group	Sweet-gum	Syca-more	Tupelo/gum	Yellow-poplar	Other hardwoods	Total hardwoods
Northeastern																
Barbour	2	15	195	--	4	34	332	432	403	231	--	0	8	1,073	42	2,867
Berkeley	--	--	75	4	0	9	36	3	150	68	--	--	0	100	1	476
Braxton	21	37	44	14	11	215	295	296	1,374	844	--	58	10	2,334	98	5,908
Grant	8	18	367	6	25	84	584	347	1,001	621	--	1	24	244	106	3,931
Hampshire	2	6	129	9	11	98	78	114	935	1,232	--	11	27	256	18	3,007
Hardy	2	13	129	11	2	69	195	167	1,035	1,019	--	8	33	241	26	3,158
Harrison	19	--	124	2	24	78	151	220	304	148	--	101	11	1,187	46	2,548
Jefferson	--	--	73	3	--	5	36	1	101	34	--	2	0	63	2	348
Lewis	5	13	38	4	6	184	158	297	701	400	--	11	15	1,683	45	3,690
Mineral	--	0	153	4	5	68	200	72	395	366	--	--	5	150	19	1,563
Morgan	2	1	72	3	1	19	51	52	363	351	--	16	9	137	10	1,122
Pendleton	10	45	324	4	2	85	401	267	1,337	788	--	3	6	363	55	3,851
Pocahontas	86	245	515	11	14	116	629	1,223	1,572	717	--	--	2	713	150	7,036
Preston	23	75	724	0	21	143	542	1,055	1,883	692	--	6	17	2,424	115	8,105
Randolph	145	322	1,198	3	7	146	1,033	2,197	1,216	907	--	0	17	2,665	332	10,809
Taylor	--	1	42	1	1	15	68	148	212	76	--	3	2	360	8	970
Tucker	127	78	660	--	32	75	413	754	1,013	537	--	2	14	2,142	124	6,369
Upshur	29	92	130	5	3	131	322	688	1,121	553	--	58	14	2,501	85	5,864
Webster	42	114	343	4	10	129	547	725	1,173	787	--	5	15	3,448	183	8,065
Unit total	524	1,077	5,334	86	179	1,703	6,070	9,058	16,290	10,372	--	286	230	22,083	1,468	79,686
Southern																
Boone	14	35	90	3	9	98	144	212	699	691	--	44	11	1,004	47	3,259
Clay	2	29	24	6	6	79	153	244	753	441	--	3	10	1,031	56	3,007
Fayette	5	54	224	21	4	291	590	983	2,619	1,913	--	17	36	3,544	149	11,168
Greenbrier	86	99	578	23	9	337	560	1,116	2,386	1,861	--	9	28	2,929	404	11,071
Kanawha	4	9	109	5	13	139	333	480	1,456	873	--	9	11	1,619	75	5,544
Logan	0	4	6	3	1	15	25	33	184	74	--	0	2	857	9	1,276
McDowell	2	4	56	11	0	43	68	220	506	254	--	1	1	2,126	6	3,468
Mercer	--	13	149	24	0	67	221	655	1,312	478	--	--	5	2,033	43	5,390
Mingo	2	1	20	6	0	16	40	54	270	135	0	0	1	877	6	1,488
Monroe	--	21	68	1	9	55	153	133	743	484	--	--	2	638	42	2,497
Nicholas	38	134	126	13	4	135	394	910	1,090	795	2	22	43	3,267	145	7,677
Raleigh	1	17	175	8	0	55	377	523	1,590	623	--	0	6	2,355	87	6,168
Summers	--	2	103	5	4	48	311	265	1,479	581	--	--	6	889	49	3,990
Wyoming	1	6	86	10	0	31	182	285	951	368	--	1	2	2,346	44	4,543
Unit total	154	429	1,813	138	60	1,408	3,550	6,115	16,038	9,572	2	105	162	25,516	1,163	70,549

Northwestern

County	(1)	(2)	(3)	(4)	(5)	(6)	(7)	(8)	(9)	(10)	(11)	(12)	(13)	(14)	(15)	Total
Brooke	—	—	27	0	4	0	23	4	36	17	—	1	0	20	3	138
Cabell	2	0	15	70	2	9	75	57	276	489	—	3	1	283	3	1,331
Calhoun	4	3	10	6	2	100	91	96	710	475	—	19	2	615	8	2,221
Doddridge	0	0	39	1	2	39	113	235	336	195	—	2	8	969	47	2,106
Gilmer	5	5	14	7	10	132	103	152	516	390	—	14	2	629	24	2,162
Hancock	—	—	8	—	0	2	1	5	2	1	—	—	0	0	0	19
Jackson	1	1	26	2	9	36	91	91	490	332	—	2	5	306	16	1,476
Lincoln	4	2	10	61	0	27	30	67	451	620	—	1	1	530	2	1,854
Marion	5	3	253	7	13	56	204	363	695	376	—	27	3	1,019	54	3,283
Marshall	—	1	67	7	39	9	44	55	80	27	—	8	0	114	14	513
Mason	2	0	18	1	3	9	50	51	243	197	—	2	0	614	5	1,242
Monongalia	6	19	469	6	36	67	254	425	837	483	—	15	4	1,760	30	4,620
Ohio	—	—	10	0	51	—	25	1	7	—	—	10	0	6	40	156
Pleasants	3	—	0	0	1	4	10	6	52	28	—	2	0	49	3	170
Putnam	—	1	15	1	9	20	60	57	355	322	—	1	8	371	36	1,341
Ritchie	3	9	70	6	12	97	126	233	901	568	—	23	13	805	30	3,053
Roane	5	4	52	4	94	135	149	524	425	—	—	28	3	768	10	2,315
Tyler	0	1	24	6	2	14	40	50	108	78	—	2	1	358	6	725
Wayne	4	2	23	63	1	22	54	134	650	744	0	2	1	913	3	2,664
Wetzel	5	7	56	3	27	43	186	164	521	300	—	26	4	1,069	52	2,625
Wirt	3	1	15	2	6	35	57	78	328	267	—	10	1	406	10	1,265
Wood	3	0	27	6	6	14	52	80	215	161	—	6	6	143	23	803
Unit total	56	57	1,249	261	239	827	1,824	2,552	8,332	6,495	0	204	62	11,746	420	36,082
State total	57	1,563	8,396	485	479	3,939	11,444	17,725	40,659	26,439	2	595	454	59,344	3,051	186,317

All table cells without observations are indicated by — . Table value of 0 indicates the volume rounds to less than 1 thousand cubic feet. Columns and rows may not add to their totals due to rounding.

Table 12.-- Sawtimber removals from timberland for industrial roundwood in thousand board feet, International 1/ 4-inch rule, by Forest Inventory Unit, county, and species group, West Virginia, 2007

Forest Inventory Unit and county	All species	Softwoods								Hardwoods			
		Eastern redcedar	Hemlock	Loblolly/ shortleaf pine	Red pine	White pine	Other pine	Spruce	Total softwoods	Ash	Aspen/ balsam poplar	Bass-wood	Beech
Northeastern													
Barbour	15,178	--	4	--	--	9	1	2	17	251	39	159	30
Berkeley	2,505	0	--	1	--	--	1	--	2	100	--	60	--
Braxton	31,221	--	9	0	--	22	9	4	44	511	--	440	290
Grant	18,992	0	7	--	--	2	15	1	25	619	49	1,376	151
Hampshire	15,816	--	82	13	--	481	627	--	1,202	240	3	126	19
Hardy	16,515	0	56	2	--	486	203	1	747	421	--	584	5
Harrison	13,348	--	0	--	--	4	0	0	5	470	33	65	81
Jefferson	1,832	--	--	--	--	--	--	--	--	106	--	46	--
Lewis	19,908	--	9	--	--	8	8	2	27	217	46	194	220
Mineral	7,848	--	33	34	--	--	330	--	397	310	--	267	--
Morgan	6,227	--	--	--	--	81	840	--	921	127	--	38	--
Pendleton	19,950	--	24	--	--	65	67	13	168	291	2	411	101
Pocahontas	35,153	--	42	68	--	198	117	56	481	1,245	147	2,718	659
Preston	41,568	--	7	--	3	20	--	1	31	552	19	762	567
Randolph	53,424	--	16	--	--	48	1	6	71	588	--	991	1,272
Taylor	5,043	--	--	--	--	--	--	--	--	123	--	36	7
Tucker	32,151	--	48	--	--	9	1	20	78	575	1	803	537
Upshur	30,518	--	9	--	--	9	9	2	28	247	--	241	203
Webster	41,752	--	12	0	--	5	10	4	31	473	76	1,352	658
Unit total	408,948	0	359	118	3	1,447	2,241	110	4,278	7,466	415	10,669	4,800
Southern													
Boone	16,944	--	2	--	--	2	1	--	5	38	--	548	187
Clay	16,025	--	10	0	--	4	5	3	23	220	--	498	139
Fayette	54,581	--	192	4	--	48	6	6	256	281	--	2,199	933
Greenbrier	50,810	0	170	49	--	125	84	5	433	894	--	780	1,117
Kanawha	29,551	--	3	--	--	4	67	2	75	779	--	1,081	244
Logan	7,354	--	--	3	--	0	14	--	17	51	--	256	11
McDowell	17,594	--	8	32	--	201	39	--	280	243	--	441	161
Mercer	26,649	--	28	35	33	450	129	0	674	376	--	802	597
Mingo	8,460	--	1	--	--	0	1	--	2	74	--	235	16
Monroe	13,069	--	--	--	--	90	369	--	459	289	--	397	69
Nicholas	37,290	--	317	0	--	48	5	6	376	373	--	1,405	722
Raleigh	31,734	--	162	--	--	19	--	4	185	487	8	989	218
Summers	20,697	--	3	--	--	80	198	--	280	539	--	668	50
Wyoming	22,967	--	2	18	--	262	--	--	282	318	--	652	167
Unit total	353,725	0	899	142	33	1,334	916	25	3,347	4,961	8	10,951	4,631

Northwestern													
Brooke	653	--	--	--	--	2	--	--	2	6	--	--	--
Cabell	7,233	--	--	--	--	--	168	2	168	191	--	40	8
Calhoun	11,945	--	3	--	--	3	9	--	17	141	8	176	98
Doddridge	11,212	--	--	--	--	53	4	--	57	236	172	77	70
Gilmer	11,536	--	3	--	--	2	14	--	20	164	--	250	426
Hancock	85	--	--	--	--	--	--	--	--	--	--	--	--
Jackson	8,061	--	--	22	--	--	395	--	417	220	4	92	35
Lincoln	10,113	--	--	--	--	0	--	--	0	96	--	138	20
Marion	16,785	--	--	--	--	1	--	--	1	393	241	273	79
Marshall	2,363	--	--	--	--	--	--	--	--	121	19	48	14
Mason	7,169	--	--	9	--	--	261	--	270	192	9	44	0
Monongalia	24,336	--	1	--	--	1	--	--	1	534	--	343	179
Ohio	659	--	--	--	--	1	--	--	1	12	--	--	11
Pleasants	910	--	--	--	--	3	1	--	4	18	21	16	3
Putnam	7,365	--	--	--	--	25	371	--	396	279	--	85	63
Ritchie	17,651	--	--	15	--	663	1,067	--	1,745	290	37	275	175
Roane	12,514	--	3	--	--	2	5	2	11	328	30	153	79
Tyler	4,160	--	--	--	--	--	47	--	47	74	17	51	34
Wayne	12,836	--	3	--	--	1	74	2	80	119	--	132	7
Wetzel	13,770	--	--	--	--	0	0	--	1	354	43	260	110
Wirt	8,930	--	--	51	--	253	1,894	--	2,198	123	--	69	60
Wood	4,545	--	--	--	--	--	403	--	403	116	87	87	19
Unit total	194,828	--	12	98	--	1,012	4,713	6	5,841	4,008	688	2,609	1,491
State total	957,502	0	1,270	357	36	3,792	7,870	141	13,466	16,435	1,111	24,229	10,922

(Table 12 continued on the next page)

(Table 12 continued)

Forest Inventory Unit and county	Yellow birch	Other birch	Black cherry	Black walnut	Elm	Hickory	Hard maple	Soft maple	Red oak group	White oak group	Sweet-gum	Syca-more	Tupelo/gum	Yellow-poplar	Other hardwoods	Total hardwoods
Northeastern																
Barbour	8	66	1,028	--	18	163	1,691	2,131	2,071	1,192	--	1	--	6,111	166	15,161
Berkeley	--	--	397	22	0	47	182	16	787	353	--	--	--	531	7	2,503
Braxton	135	163	228	84	49	1,045	1,481	1,422	7,130	4,328	--	254	49	13,157	410	31,177
Grant	38	73	1,853	39	102	370	2,807	1,587	5,056	3,017	--	2	99	1,289	441	18,967
Hampshire	15	26	674	57	43	415	393	514	4,666	5,841	--	46	109	1,355	73	14,613
Hardy	11	59	685	73	8	312	977	797	5,248	4,997	--	36	147	1,290	120	15,768
Harrison	128	--	642	11	99	360	755	1,034	1,571	771	--	423	48	6,667	184	13,343
Jefferson	--	--	386	18	--	26	182	3	530	181	--	10	--	334	9	1,832
Lewis	31	61	200	23	27	926	811	1,435	3,651	2,095	--	52	69	9,650	174	19,881
Mineral	--	2	773	25	20	287	940	320	1,935	1,683	--	--	19	791	78	7,451
Morgan	9	6	377	16	5	82	251	220	1,724	1,536	--	64	34	778	42	5,306
Pendleton	49	211	1,718	25	11	416	2,035	1,337	6,929	4,031	--	13	31	1,924	246	19,782
Pocahontas	428	1,046	2,720	65	60	566	3,186	5,561	8,233	3,681	--	--	9	3,728	619	34,672
Preston	114	331	3,684	1	98	687	2,669	5,002	9,715	3,552	--	27	71	13,196	488	41,537
Randolph	663	1,337	6,032	22	28	669	5,045	9,987	6,153	4,487	--	1	69	14,645	1,364	53,352
Taylor	--	5	210	4	5	72	336	708	1,101	391	--	17	8	1,986	35	5,043
Tucker	533	328	3,312	--	142	373	2,033	3,629	5,187	2,727	--	11	56	11,347	479	32,073
Upshur	162	383	680	31	15	655	1,631	3,171	5,833	2,874	--	228	57	13,727	353	30,490
Webster	209	490	1,827	22	48	646	2,790	3,386	6,094	4,044	--	24	64	18,791	726	41,721
Unit total	2,533	4,587	27,426	537	777	8,117	30,194	42,259	83,614	51,781	--	1,209	974	121,298	6,015	404,670
Southern																
Boone	94	150	475	17	37	510	730	1,008	3,587	3,557	--	187	46	5,574	193	16,939
Clay	11	127	129	35	27	418	784	1,145	3,953	2,324	--	14	43	5,890	247	16,002
Fayette	29	225	1,116	89	21	1,361	2,906	4,402	13,352	9,538	--	75	148	17,011	639	54,326
Greenbrier	354	404	2,651	111	38	1,417	2,674	4,850	11,437	8,370	--	37	113	13,482	1,648	50,377
Kanawha	26	44	575	32	54	725	1,700	2,395	7,660	4,551	--	41	46	9,183	341	29,477
Logan	2	19	32	17	3	82	128	161	968	388	--	1	7	5,173	38	7,337
McDowell	14	17	280	57	1	218	345	985	2,678	1,315	--	2	5	10,527	25	17,314
Mercer	--	52	715	99	2	291	1,108	2,790	6,761	2,378	--	--	20	9,788	196	25,975
Mingo	12	5	131	41	1	83	203	274	1,421	707	0	1	3	5,226	24	8,457
Monroe	--	87	352	5	36	235	766	645	3,777	2,359	--	--	6	3,401	185	12,610
Nicholas	172	558	596	62	19	620	1,900	3,989	5,513	3,857	9	92	173	16,243	615	36,915
Raleigh	6	72	953	36	2	254	1,857	2,436	8,192	3,127	--	2	26	12,505	381	31,549
Summers	--	9	540	29	14	210	1,566	1,302	7,640	2,930	--	--	27	4,663	230	20,417
Wyoming	5	25	440	47	2	133	924	1,276	4,946	1,863	--	2	6	11,679	201	22,685
Unit total	725	1,794	8,984	677	255	6,558	17,591	27,658	81,882	47,263	9	454	670	130,343	4,964	350,378

Northwestern

County														Total
Brooke	--	127	0	6	1	107	19	180	83	3	2	107	9	650
Cabell	15	81	436	8	39	379	289	1,442	2,545	11	3	1,566	14	7,066
Calhoun	25	53	40	11	532	465	486	3,734	2,496	101	10	3,502	36	11,928
Doddridge	2	203	9	8	170	560	1,085	1,724	980	11	34	5,628	184	11,155
Gilmer	32	72	43	43	701	527	748	2,701	2,049	66	9	3,561	101	11,515
Hancock	--	36	--	0	9	4	24	9	3	--	--	--	--	85
Jackson	5	136	15	37	175	461	438	2,547	1,691	10	21	1,683	67	7,644
Lincoln	30	53	382	0	145	151	341	2,371	3,266	5	3	3,089	12	10,112
Marion	35	1,320	45	56	267	1,025	1,712	3,603	1,933	108	10	5,450	219	16,784
Marshall	--	331	33	129	35	206	239	404	131	29	2	572	48	2,363
Mason	16	97	7	12	43	253	258	1,272	1,024	7	1	3,644	21	6,899
Monongalia	35	2,431	40	157	345	1,280	2,059	4,349	2,515	66	15	9,771	129	24,335
Ohio	--	47	0	193	--	120	4	34	--	39	--	42	155	658
Pleasants	21	2	0	5	18	53	28	272	155	9	0	269	14	906
Putnam	--	80	7	36	95	305	274	1,841	1,649	7	31	2,068	143	6,968
Ritchie	21	395	37	51	487	635	1,097	4,698	2,932	107	52	4,456	123	15,906
Roane	36	278	23	16	498	692	748	2,752	2,235	142	13	4,416	47	12,503
Tyler	2	129	41	10	71	202	243	567	405	9	5	2,227	25	4,113
Wayne	31	120	397	3	113	276	571	2,931	3,372	9	5	4,649	14	12,756
Wetzel	33	292	13	98	183	917	766	2,704	1,547	109	15	6,097	195	13,769
Wirt	21	78	14	25	173	288	382	1,701	1,362	44	3	2,343	42	6,731
Wood	19	141	40	24	72	265	384	1,126	843	27	23	776	92	4,142
Unit total	378	6,501	1,622	929	4,172	9,172	12,195	42,961	33,215	918	258	65,916	1,690	188,988
State total	3,636	42,912	2,836	1,962	18,846	56,957	82,112	208,457	132,259	2,581	1,902	317,557	12,669	944,036

All table cells without observations are indicated by -- . Table value of 0 indicates the volume rounds to less than 1 thousand board feet. Columns and rows may not add to their totals due to rounding.

Table 13.-- Harvest residue generated by industrial roundwood harvesting in thousand cubic feet, by Forest Inventory Unit, county, and species group, West Virginia, 2007

Forest Inventory Unit and county	All species	Softwoods								Hardwoods			
		Eastern redcedar	Hemlock	Loblolly/ shortleaf pine	Red pine	White pine	Other pine	Spruce	Total softwoods	Ash	Aspen/ balsam poplar	Bass-wood	Beech
Northeastern													
Barbour	1,650	--	3	--	--	7	1	1	12	33	3	17	4
Berkeley	338	0	--	0	--	--	0	--	0	14	--	8	--
Braxton	3,185	--	6	0	--	12	4	3	24	65	--	44	29
Grant	2,008	0	2	--	--	1	6	0	10	69	1	80	9
Hampshire	1,773	--	20	3	--	115	154	--	293	27	0	13	1
Hardy	1,984	0	14	1	--	120	52	0	187	53	--	57	1
Harrison	1,240	--	0	--	--	3	0	0	3	59	1	9	8
Jefferson	246	--	--	--	--	--	--	--	--	13	--	6	--
Lewis	2,088	--	6	--	--	6	5	2	19	30	1	28	31
Mineral	822	--	8	8	--	--	82	--	98	29	--	20	--
Morgan	669	--	--	--	--	20	204	--	224	11	--	5	--
Pendleton	2,585	--	7	--	--	37	40	4	88	38	0	44	11
Pocahontas	3,928	--	13	18	--	77	31	22	160	165	3	171	76
Preston	4,699	--	4	--	1	6	--	0	11	76	0	86	59
Randolph	4,995	--	10	--	--	16	1	5	32	68	--	81	105
Taylor	564	--	--	--	--	--	--	--	--	17	--	4	1
Tucker	3,520	--	26	--	--	7	1	10	43	72	0	88	43
Upshur	3,040	--	6	--	--	5	6	1	18	31	--	30	27
Webster	4,294	--	9	0	--	4	7	3	22	64	3	100	81
Unit total	43,630	0	135	30	1	436	593	51	1,246	934	13	892	487
Southern													
Boone	1,802	--	0	--	--	0	0	--	1	5	--	59	24
Clay	1,704	--	5	0	--	3	3	2	13	31	--	51	20
Fayette	5,260	--	46	1	--	13	2	2	64	36	--	264	48
Greenbrier	3,956	0	41	12	--	31	20	2	106	66	--	71	39
Kanawha	3,442	--	2	--	--	2	17	1	22	110	--	123	31
Logan	639	--	--	--	--	0	3	--	4	7	--	24	1
McDowell	1,583	--	2	--	--	50	9	--	69	33	--	54	4
Mercer	2,650	--	6	9	8	102	30	0	155	48	--	86	13
Mingo	836	--	0	--	--	0	0	--	1	11	--	26	2
Monroe	1,595	--	78	--	--	14	87	--	101	38	--	52	5
Nicholas	3,135	--	78	0	--	13	3	3	96	42	--	103	41
Raleigh	3,379	--	38	--	--	4	--	1	43	61	0	117	8
Summers	2,646	--	1	--	--	11	47	--	58	69	--	89	3
Wyoming	2,232	--	0	4	--	56	--	--	61	45	--	84	5
Unit total	34,858	0	220	35	8	299	221	11	794	602	0	1,203	244

Northwestern

County													
Brooke	88	—	—	—	—	0	—	—	0	1	—	—	—
Cabell	885	—	—	—	—	2	41	—	41	26	6	1	1
Calhoun	1,472	—	2	—	—	13	3	1	8	20	22	0	14
Doddridge	949	—	—	—	—	2	1	—	14	31	8	4	5
Gilmer	1,320	—	2	—	—	—	5	1	9	22	31	—	61
Hancock	12	—	—	5	—	—	—	—	—	—	—	0	—
Jackson	988	—	—	—	—	0	98	—	103	30	12	—	4
Lincoln	1,175	—	—	—	—	0	—	—	0	14	19	5	3
Marion	1,913	—	—	—	—	—	—	—	0	50	30	0	10
Marshall	267	—	—	2	—	—	—	—	—	16	5	0	2
Mason	774	—	0	—	—	—	64	—	67	27	6	—	0
Monongalia	2,725	—	—	0	—	0	—	—	0	64	40	—	25
Ohio	40	—	—	—	—	—	0	—	0	2	1	1	2
Pleasants	108	—	—	—	—	1	—	—	1	3	1	—	0
Putnam	851	—	—	—	—	6	92	—	98	37	9	—	6
Ritchie	2,202	—	2	4	—	164	264	—	431	38	26	1	19
Roane	1,484	—	—	—	—	2	2	1	6	47	20	1	11
Tyler	376	—	2	2	—	—	12	—	12	10	5	0	4
Wayne	1,530	—	—	0	—	1	17	1	21	17	18	—	1
Wetzel	1,432	—	—	—	—	0	0	1	0	50	22	1	16
Wirt	1,271	—	—	13	—	63	468	—	543	17	10	—	8
Wood	593	—	—	—	—	—	100	—	100	16	10	2	3
Unit total	22,454	—	8	24	8	253	1,166	5	1,455	537	299	16	193
State total	100,942	0	362	89	8	988	1,980	67	3,495	2,074	2,394	30	924

(Table 13 continued on the next page)

55

(Table 13 continued)

Forest Inventory Unit and county	Yellow birch	Other birch	Black cherry	Black walnut	Elm	Hickory	Hard maple	Soft maple	Red oak group	White oak group	Sweet-gum	Syca-more	Tupelo/gum	Yellow-poplar	Other hardwoods	Total hardwoods
Northeastern																
Barbour	1	5	136	--	2	19	223	263	261	150	--	0	2	506	11	1,637
Berkeley	--	--	56	1	0	6	25	2	103	46	--	--	5	75	1	338
Braxton	7	11	31	3	4	126	189	160	879	533	--	17	5	1,034	24	3,161
Grant	3	3	229	1	4	30	309	145	598	316	--	0	4	175	21	1,998
Hampshire	1	1	92	2	1	22	53	44	531	557	--	1	3	129	3	1,480
Hardy	0	5	97	2	0	28	126	86	627	536	--	3	10	154	10	1,796
Harrison	5	--	83	0	4	41	97	107	201	99	--	22	3	489	9	1,237
Jefferson	--	--	55	1	--	4	25	0	69	24	--	1	--	47	1	246
Lewis	3	6	28	1	2	126	111	164	473	274	--	5	6	772	7	2,068
Mineral	--	0	97	1	0	15	94	26	209	142	--	--	1	89	3	724
Morgan	1	0	52	1	0	5	30	12	162	100	--	2	1	62	1	446
Pendleton	3	20	230	1	1	52	268	172	860	495	--	1	3	273	23	2,497
Pocahontas	50	61	339	2	3	71	409	494	1,027	457	--	--	0	412	29	3,769
Preston	13	23	468	0	11	78	328	545	1,194	442	--	2	3	1,329	31	4,689
Randolph	57	61	644	1	1	65	580	886	723	500	--	0	3	1,113	74	4,963
Taylor	--	0	29	0	1	9	45	80	142	49	--	2	0	182	2	564
Tucker	26	17	388	--	11	45	248	409	640	328	--	1	2	1,136	22	3,477
Upshur	14	17	94	1	1	84	218	300	749	366	--	5	3	1,060	20	3,023
Webster	25	29	233	1	4	85	366	340	770	509	--	2	3	1,622	35	4,272
Unit total	208	262	3,380	19	51	912	3,744	4,236	10,219	5,922	--	66	53	10,660	326	42,384
Southern																
Boone	3	9	67	1	1	72	100	116	470	466	--	11	2	387	9	1,802
Clay	2	9	18	1	2	59	108	117	518	302	--	2	2	430	18	1,691
Fayette	2	11	134	2	2	131	358	364	1,616	1,091	--	5	6	1,087	39	5,196
Greenbrier	15	16	217	3	2	71	292	335	1,099	637	--	2	4	917	62	3,849
Kanawha	1	5	81	1	3	96	229	305	979	582	--	4	3	840	29	3,420
Logan	0	1	4	1	0	12	18	18	127	51	--	0	0	369	2	635
McDowell	0	1	33	2	0	28	46	80	328	166	--	0	0	736	2	1,515
Mercer	--	1	76	2	0	26	146	175	855	286	--	--	1	762	17	2,494
Mingo	1	0	6	1	0	12	28	37	186	93	0	0	0	432	2	836
Monroe	--	4	48	0	1	19	98	80	460	254	--	--	0	422	12	1,494
Nicholas	11	27	60	2	2	56	205	291	658	398	0	5	6	1,098	34	3,038
Raleigh	0	4	102	1	0	26	242	258	1,046	386	--	0	2	1,056	27	3,335
Summers	--	0	74	1	0	23	208	166	977	360	--	--	2	594	22	2,588
Wyoming	0	1	56	1	0	16	126	114	635	237	0	0	0	833	17	2,171
Unit total	34	89	977	20	14	647	2,203	2,455	9,954	5,310	0	29	29	9,964	291	34,065

Northwestern

County																Total
Brooke	--	--	18	0	1	0	14	3	24	11	--	0	0	15	1	87
Cabell	0	0	11	16	1	4	50	38	187	325	--	1	0	179	1	844
Calhoun	1	2	8	1	1	75	64	65	488	327	--	14	1	359	3	1,464
Doddridge	0	0	27	0	0	13	71	103	214	114	--	1	1	338	5	935
Gilmer	1	2	10	2	2	99	73	92	353	269	--	5	1	281	6	1,310
Hancock	--	--	5	--	0	1	1	3	1	0	--	--	--	--	--	12
Jackson	0	1	19	1	0	20	60	50	313	202	--	1	1	166	4	885
Lincoln	1	1	7	14	0	20	21	46	311	422	--	1	0	294	2	1,175
Marion	1	2	180	2	3	28	133	178	454	240	--	4	0	586	8	1,913
Marshall	--	0	41	1	4	5	28	24	53	17	--	1	0	68	2	267
Mason	0	0	14	0	0	5	34	34	165	129	--	0	0	291	1	707
Monongalia	3	8	305	1	10	45	168	239	555	322	--	5	0	925	8	2,725
Ohio	--	--	7	0	4	--	15	0	4	--	--	1	1	1	4	40
Pleasants	1	--	0	0	0	3	7	4	36	17	--	1	0	33	1	107
Putnam	--	1	11	0	1	11	41	31	234	200	--	1	1	167	5	754
Ritchie	1	2	38	1	3	60	83	115	590	363	--	10	2	414	4	1,771
Roane	1	2	40	1	1	70	95	97	361	293	--	19	1	413	4	1,477
Tyler	0	0	18	1	0	9	27	28	74	52	--	1	0	133	1	364
Wayne	1	1	17	15	0	15	38	76	374	435	0	9	0	500	1	1,509
Wetzel	1	2	41	0	2	25	125	86	354	198	--	9	0	492	8	1,431
Wirt	1	1	11	1	1	21	38	46	216	164	--	4	0	188	2	728
Wood	0	0	20	1	1	10	36	43	147	108	--	1	1	91	3	494
Unit total	12	25	848	59	39	537	1,221	1,400	5,507	4,208	0	80	12	5,932	74	20,999
State total	254	376	5,204	98	103	2,097	7,168	8,091	25,679	15,440	0	174	94	26,556	691	97,447

All table cells without observations are indicated by --. Table value of 0 indicates the volume rounds to less than 1 thousand cubic feet. Columns and rows may not add to their totals due to rounding.

Table 14. -- Disposition of residues produced at primary wood-using mills in thousand tons, green weight, by Forest Inventory Unit, disposition, residue type, and softwoods and hardwoods, West Virginia, 2007

Forest Inventory Unit and disposition	Total all residues		Residue type							
			Total wood residue		Wood residue				Bark	
					Coarse		Fine			
	Softwood	Hardwood	Softwood	Hardwood	Softwood	Hardwood	Softwood	Hardwood	Softwood	Hardwood
All Units										
Fiber products	13.34	1,083.69	12.88	1,064.15	6.93	922.98	5.95	141.18	0.46	19.54
Charcoal	2.29	138.00	1.06	69.32	0.18	23.98	0.88	45.33	1.23	68.68
Industrial fuel	13.69	403.54	4.31	231.56	0.12	77.15	4.18	154.41	9.38	171.98
Domestic fuel	0.78	22.36	0.66	19.44	0.34	12.54	0.32	6.91	0.12	2.92
Mulch	6.06	254.60	0.90	1.05	0.85	1.05	0.05	--	5.16	253.55
Wood pellets	--	68.81	--	68.81	--	29.45	--	39.36	--	--
Miscellaneous[a]	1.82	88.02	0.44	28.32	--	11.14	0.44	17.18	1.38	59.70
Not used	1.55	20.27	0.96	15.31	0.82	8.90	0.14	6.41	0.59	4.96
Unit total	39.54	2,079.30	21.22	1,497.96	9.25	1,087.17	11.96	410.79	18.32	581.34
Northeastern										
Fiber products	4.76	498.38	4.30	478.84	1.88	416.27	2.42	62.56	0.46	19.54
Charcoal	2.25	109.41	1.02	54.24	0.18	22.80	0.84	31.44	1.23	55.17
Industrial fuel	6.22	235.37	2.08	142.63	--	71.91	2.08	70.71	4.14	92.74
Domestic fuel	0.32	6.73	0.20	4.97	0.17	4.23	0.03	0.74	0.12	1.76
Mulch	2.08	88.85	--	--	--	--	--	--	2.08	88.85
Wood pellets	--	21.58	--	21.58	--	--	--	21.58	--	--
Miscellaneous[a]	1.28	31.87	0.31	4.65	--	0.39	0.31	4.26	0.97	27.22
Not used	1.15	4.50	0.90	3.23	0.80	2.34	0.10	0.88	0.25	1.27
Unit total	18.07	996.69	8.82	710.13	3.04	517.96	5.78	192.17	9.25	286.56
Southern										
Fiber products	8.58	495.48	8.58	495.48	5.05	427.82	3.53	67.65	--	--
Charcoal	0.04	26.78	0.04	13.27	--	--	0.04	13.27	--	13.51
Industrial fuel	7.42	153.64	2.18	74.94	0.08	2.06	2.10	72.89	5.24	78.70
Domestic fuel	0.29	2.37	0.29	2.12	--	1.81	0.29	0.31	--	0.25
Mulch	3.90	145.76	0.85	0.07	0.85	0.07	--	--	3.05	145.69
Wood pellets	--	45.55	--	45.55	--	29.45	--	16.10	--	--
Miscellaneous[a]	0.37	11.33	0.04	1.33	--	--	0.04	1.33	0.33	10.00
Not used	0.34	6.57	0.04	4.47	0.02	2.85	0.02	1.62	0.30	2.10
Unit total	20.94	887.47	12.02	637.23	6.00	464.06	6.02	173.17	8.92	250.24
Northwestern										
Fiber products	--	89.84	--	89.84	--	78.88	--	10.96	--	--
Charcoal	--	1.81	--	1.81	--	1.18	--	0.63	--	--
Industrial fuel	0.04	14.53	0.04	13.99	0.04	3.18	--	10.81	--	0.54
Domestic fuel	0.17	13.26	0.17	12.35	0.17	6.50	--	5.86	--	0.91
Mulch	0.09	19.99	0.05	0.97	--	0.97	0.05	--	0.04	19.02
Wood pellets	--	1.68	--	1.68	--	--	--	1.68	--	--
Miscellaneous[a]	0.17	44.81	0.10	22.33	--	10.74	0.10	11.59	0.07	22.48
Not used	0.06	9.21	0.02	7.62	--	3.70	0.02	3.92	0.04	1.59
Unit total	0.53	195.15	0.38	150.61	0.22	105.16	0.17	45.45	0.15	44.54

[a] Livestock bedding, small dimension, and specialty items.
All table cells without observations are indicated by --. Columns and rows may not add to their totals due to rounding.